Cancellation of Removal for Lawful Permanent Residents

Keeping the Green Card after Committing a Crime

Attorney Brian D. Lerner

LAW OFFICES OF
BRIAN D. LERNER
A PROFESSIONAL CORPORATION

ATTORNEY DRAFTED IMMIGRATION PETITIONS

By

Brian D. Lerner

Attorney at Law

Disclaimer and Terms of Use:

Effort has been made to ensure that the information in this book is accurate and complete. However, the author and the publisher do not warrant that this particular petition will mirror or be exactly as your situation. There has not been any attorney-client agreement created by the purchase of this petition or application. No legal advice has occurred. The cases, regulations and/or statutes cited may change at any time without notice.

ISBN: 978-1-958990-12-4

INTRODUCTION

There are a multitude of different immigration petitions and applications. They are complex and full of requirements. Obviously, it would be best to hire an immigration attorney to best prepare the petitions and applications. However, this can certainly cost thousands of dollars.

The next best option is to get a sample of the petition written by an experienced immigration attorney. The samples cost a fraction what would be charged by an immigration attorney. However, while the reader has to alter, amend and change the parts of the sample petition to reflect their actual situation, it is a fantastic roadmap for them to use. If the reader has purchased the entire petition or application, they will have real live samples of cover letters, forms, declarations, affidavits and the necessary exhibits to use. The samples come from real cases and the names of those clients have been redacted to protect the privacy of that person or corporation.

These are petitions and applications that have been drafted by an experienced immigration attorney with over 25 years of experience. Get the benefits of that experience without the costs.

CONTENTS

About the Law Offices of Brian D. Lerner

Brian D. Lerner has been a licensed attorney since 1992 and started the Law Offices of Brian D. Lerner, APC. The law practice consists of Immigration and Nationality Law and everything involved with and regarding immigration which includes citizenship, investment visas, family and employment visas, removal and deportation hearings, appeals, waivers, adjustment, consulate processing and all types of immigration and citizenship matters. Thousands of families have been reunited and/or permitted to stay in the U.S. and/or return to the U.S. because of the successful work of Immigration Attorney Brian D. Lerner.

This law offices handles all types of immigration cases including family based and employment based. Immigration issues range from immigration court proceedings to trying to fix what paralegals may have done that was neither correct nor proper. Foreign nationals must have experience lawyers admitted to practice law.

The Law Offices of Brian D. Lerner, APC, handles cases arising from business visas, work permits, Green Cards, non-immigrant visas, deportation, citizenship, appeals and all areas of immigration. The Law Offices of Brian D. Lerner, APC does EB-5 Investor Visas, H-1B Specialty Occupation, L-1 Intracompany Transferee, E-2 Treaty Investor, E-1 Treaty Trader, O-1 Extraordinary Ability among others. Regarding immigrant visas for the Green Card, the firm does PERM and advanced degree PERM, Family Petitions, and Extraordinary Alien Petitions. In addition to affirmative petitions, the Law Firm represents people in people in deportation and removal hearings, including political asylum, withholding of removal, and convention against torture cases.

Brian D. Lerner has been certified as an expert in Immigration & Nationality Law by the California State Bar, Board of Legal Specialization since 2000 and has been re-certified three times. He now passes on his decades of experience by allowing the Reader, Law Schools, Professors and other Immigration Attorneys to purchase sample petitions on every facet of Immigration Law.

About a Legal Permanent Resident Cancellation (42A)

A Legal Permanent Resident may have his removal cancelled before a hearing before an Immigration Judge. In order for this to happen, the Legal Permanent Resident has had this status for 5 years, he has had at least 7 years continuous residence in the United States after having been lawfully admitted in any status, and has not been convicted of an aggravated felony. Also has the Form EOIR-42A attached.

Do you already have your Green Card, but committed a crime and now U.S. Immigration is trying to deport you? This is possible, but you may qualify for a form of relief which for all intense purposes is your 'get out of jail' free card. A Lawful Permanent Resident or somebody with a Green Card may have his removal cancelled before a hearing before an Immigration Judge. In order for this to happen, the Legal Permanent Resident has had this status for 5 years, he has had at least 7 years continuous residence in the United States after having been lawfully admitted in any status, and has not been convicted of an aggravated felony. Also has the Form EOIR-42A attached.

Many times, people who are not in Removal Proceedings or Deportation Proceedings believe that they can do cancellation of removal applications. In fact, many foreign nationals not in immigration court think that all they must do is remain in the U.S. for 10 years and voila that they qualify.

Unfortunately, it is not that easy, nor is it correct. The Cancellation of Removal for Lawful Permanent Residents is quite a bit easier to get approved than the other Cancellation of Removal for those people who don't have their Green Cards. It is not easy, but much easier. For this Cancellation of Removal, you need to have been physically present in the United States for 7 years and have had residency for 5 years and to have not been convicted of an aggravated felon. Thus, you do not need to show good moral character and you do not need to show extreme hardship to a U.S. relative such as a child, spouse or parent. Even if you have an aggravated felon, you may be able to go back to criminal court to argue why the sentence should be reduced or the guilty plea vacated.

Cancellation of Removal or 'Cancellation of Deportation' for people who have Green Cards, is basically a get out of jail free card. Once you prepare the application, argue the merits hearing in front of the Immigration Judge and await a decision, you will get your Green Card back and get removal proceedings ended if you win.

The sample Cancellation of Removal packet for Lawful Permanent Residents you see will give lots of great information and a significant amount of information and data that will comply with the requirements. Thus, if you cannot hire an immigration lawyer to prepare the necessary Cancellation of Removal Packet, this is the next best thing. Follow it carefully and closely and you will have a real chance of realizing your dream to stay inside the United States. Note that the Immigration judge nor the trial attorney from the department of homeland security are your friend, and you must properly either get legal representation via an attorney or represent yourself. Either way, if you qualify for this, you must make it as strong as possible.

ATTORNEY COVER LETTER

Brian D. Lerner (Bar No. 158536)
Christopher A. Reed (Bar No. 235438)
Law Offices of Brian D. Lerner, APC
3233 E. Broadway
Long Beach, California 90803
Telephone: (562) 495-0554
Facsimile: (562) 608-8672

Attorneys for Respondent

UNITED STATES DEPARTMENT OF JUSTICE

EXECUTIVE OFFICE FOR IMMIGRATION REVIEW

IMMIGRATION COURT

LOS ANGELES, CALIFORNIA

In the Matter of:

███████████████████   File No: ███████████

Respondent,

In Removal Proceedings.

Immigration Judge: Monica Little   Master September 24, 2014 at 8:00 a.m.

APPLICATION FOR CANCELLATION OF REMOVAL FOR CERTAIN PERMANENT RESIDENTS AND SUPPORTING DOCUMENTS

TABLE OF CONTENTS

Form:	Description:	
EOIR-42A	Application for Cancellation of Removal for Certain Permanent Residents and Receipt Notice	

FORM EOIR-42A

Application for Cancellation of Removal for Certain Permanent Residents and Receipt Notice

U.S. Department of Justice
Executive Office for Immigration Review

Application for Cancellation of Removal for Certain Permanent Residents

---

PLEASE READ ADVICE AND INSTRUCTIONS
BEFORE FILLING IN FORM

PLEASE TYPE OR PRINT

Fee Stamp (Official Use Only)

PART 1 - INFORMATION ABOUT YOURSELF

1) My present true name is: (Last, First, Middle)	2) Alien Registration (or "A") Number(s):
▮▮▮▮▮	▮▮▮

3) My name given at birth was: (Last, First, Middle)	4) Birth Place: (City and Country)
▮▮▮▮▮	Mauban Phillipines

5) Date of Birth: (Month, Day, Year) 01/26/1979	6) Gender: ☐ Male ☒ Female	7) Height: 5'2"	8) Hair Color: Black	9) Eye Color: Brown

10) Current Nationality and Citizenship: Philippines Philippines	11) Social Security Number: ▮▮▮	12) Home Phone Number: ▮▮▮	13) Work Phone Number: ▮▮▮

14) I currently reside at: ▮	15) I have been known by these additional name(s):
Apt. number and/or in care of ▮▮▮ Number and Street Los Angeles CA 90026 City or Town State Zip Code	N/A

16) I have resided in the following locations in the United States: (List PRESENT ADDRESS FIRST, and work back in time for at least 7 years.)

Street and Number - Apt. or Room # - City or Town - State - Zip Code	Resided From: (Month, Day, Year)	Resided To: (Month, Day, Year)
▮▮▮▮▮	10/2006	PRESENT

PART 2 - INFORMATION ABOUT THIS APPLICATION

17) I, the undersigned, hereby request that my removal be cancelled under the provisions of section 240A(a) of the Immigration and Nationality Act (INA). I believe that I am eligible for this relief because I have been a lawful permanent resident alien for 5 or more years, have 7 years of continuous residence in the United States, and have not been convicted of an aggravated felony. I was admitted as or adjusted to the status of an alien lawfully admitted for permanent residence on 02/11/1989 _____

(Date)

at Los Angeles, CA _____

(Place)

3847

PART 3 - INFORMATION ABOUT YOUR PRESENCE IN THE UNITED STATES

18) My first arrival into the United States was under the name of: (Last, First, Middle)	19) My first arrival to the United States was on: (Month, Day, Year)
▅▅▅▅▅▅▅▅▅	02/11/1989

20) Place or port of first arrival: (Place or Port, City, and State)

LAX, Los Angeles, CA

21) I: ☒ was inspected and admitted.

    ☒ I entered using my Lawful Permanent Resident card which is valid until _____ .
                                                                           (Month, Day, Year)

    ☐ I entered using a _____ visa which is valid until _____
                              (Specify Type of Visa)   (Month, Day, Year)

  ☐ was not inspected and admitted.

    ☐ I entered without documents. Explain: _____
    ☐ I entered without inspection. Explain: _____

  ☐ Other. Explain:

22) I applied on _____ for additional time to stay and it was ☐ granted on _____
             (Month, Day, Year)   (Month, Day, Year)

and valid until _____ , or ☐ denied on _____ .
        (Month, Day, Year)   (Month, Day, Year)

23) Since the date of my first entry, I departed from and returned to the United States at the following places and on the following dates:
(Please list all departures regardless of how briefly you were absent from the United States.)
If you have never departed from the United States since your original date of entry, please mark an X in this box: ☐

	Port of Departure (Place or Port, City and State)	Departure Date (Month, Day, Year)	Purpose of Travel	Destination
1	MIA	06/2018 2012	Vacation	Bahamas
	Port of Return (Place or Port, City and State)	Return Date (Month, Day, Year)	Manner of Return	Inspected and Admitted?
	MIA	06/2018 2012	Air	☒ Yes ☐ No
2	Port of Departure (Place or Port, City and State)	Departure Date (Month, Day, Year)	Purpose of Travel	Destination
	LAX	1997	Vacation	Philippines
	Port of Return (Place or Port, City and State)	Return Date (Month, Day, Year)	Manner of Return	Inspected and Admitted?
	LAX	1997	Air	☒ Yes ☐ No

24) Have you ever departed the United States: a) under an order of deportation, exclusion, or removal? .... ☐ Yes ☒ No

                                        b) pursuant to a grant of voluntary departure? .... ☐ Yes ☒ No

PART 4 - INFORMATION ABOUT YOUR MARITAL STATUS AND SPOUSE (Continued on page 3)

25) I am not married: ☒ I am married: ☐	26) If married, the name of my spouse is: (Last, First, Middle)	27) My spouse's name before marriage was:

28) The marriage took place in: (City and Country)	29) Date of marriage: (Month, Day, Year)

30) My spouse currently resides at:	31) Place and date of birth of my spouse: (City & Country, Month, Day, Year)
Apt. number and/or in care of	
Number and Street	32) My spouse is a citizen of: (Country)
City or Town _State/Country_ _Zip Code_	

33) If your spouse is other than a native born United States citizen, answer the following:

He/she arrived in the United States at: (Place or Port, City and State) ....

He/she arrived in the United States on: (Month, Day, Year) ....

His/her alien registration number(s) is: A# ....

He/she was naturalized on: (Month, Day, Year) .... at ....
                                                             (City and State)

34) My spouse ☐ - is ☐ - is not employed. If employed, please give salary and the name and address of the place(s) of employment.

Full Name and Address of Employer	Earnings Per Week (Approximate)
	$
	$
	$

PART 4 - INFORMATION ABOUT YOUR MARITAL STATUS AND SPOUSE (Continued)

35) I ☐ - have ☒ - have not been previously married: (*If previously married, list the name of each prior spouse, the dates on which each marriage began and ended, the place where the marriage terminated, and describe how each marriage ended.*)

Name of prior spouse: (*Last, First, Middle*)	Date marriage began: Date marriage ended:	Place marriage ended: (*City and Country*)	Description or manner of how marriage was terminated or ended:

Name of prior spouse: (*Last, First, Middle*)	Date marriage began: Date marriage ended:	Place marriage ended: (*City and Country*)	Description or manner of how marriage was terminated or ended:

36) Have you been ordered by any court, or are otherwise under any legal obligation, to provide child support and/or spousal maintenance as a result of a separation and/or divorce? ☐ - Yes ☒ - No

PART 5 - INFORMATION ABOUT YOUR EMPLOYMENT AND FINANCIAL STATUS

37) Since my arrival into the United States, I have been employed by the following named persons or firms: (*Please begin with present employment and work back in time. Any periods of unemployment or school attendance should be specified. Attach a separate sheet for additional entries if necessary.*)

Full Name and Address of Employer	Earnings Per Week (*Approximate*)	Type of Work Performed	Employed From: (*Month, Day, Year*)	Employed To: (*Month, Day, Year*)
███████████████	$ 500	Caregiver	2011	PRESENT 2014
███████████████	$ 250	Hostess/Dealer	2000	2002
███████████████	$ 150	Cashier	1993	1993

38) If self-employed, describe the nature of the business, the name of the business, its address, and net income derived therefrom:

39) My assets (and if married, my spouse's assets) in the United States and other countries, not including clothing and household necessities, are:

Self

Cash, Stocks, and Bonds............ $ 0

Real Estate................................. $ 0

Auto (dollar value minus amount owed)...... $ 0

Other (describe on line below).............. $ 0

0 _____ TOTAL $

Jointly Owned With Spouse

Cash, Stocks, and Bonds............... $

Real Estate.................................. $

Auto (dollar value minus amount owed)........ $

Other (describe on line below)............. $

_____ TOTAL $

40) I ☒ - have ☐ - have not received public or private relief or assistance (e.g. Welfare, Unemployment Benefits, Medicaid, TANF, AFDC, etc.). If you have, please give full details including the type of relief or assistance received, date for which relief or assistance was received, place, and total amount received during this time:

2010-2012 - Food Stamps and Cash Aid

41) Please list each of the years in which you have filed an income tax return with the Internal Revenue Service: _____

2000-2002

PART 6 - INFORMATION ABOUT YOUR FAMILY (Continued on page 5)

42) I have _____ 0 _____ (Number of) children. Please list information for each child below, include assets and earnings information for children over the age of 16 who have separate incomes:

Name of Child: (Last, First, Middle) Child's Alien Registration Number:	Citizen of What Country: Birth Date: (Month, Day, Year)	Now Residing At: (City and Country) Birth Date: (City and Country)	Immigration Status of Child
A#: _____			
Estimated Total of Assets: $_____	Estimated Average Weekly Earnings: $_____		
A#: _____			
Estimated Total of Assets: $_____	Estimated Average Weekly Earnings: $_____		
A#: _____			
Estimated Total of Assets: $_____	Estimated Average Weekly Earnings: $_____		

43) If your application is denied, would your spouse and all of your children accompany you to your:

Country of Birth - ☐ Yes ☐ No

Country of Nationality - ☐ Yes ☐ No

Country of Last Residence - ☐ Yes ☐ No

If you answered "No" to any of the responses, please explain: _____

N/A

44) Members of my family, including my spouse and/or child(ren) ☐ - have ☒ - have not received public or private relief or assistance (e.g., Welfare, Unemployment Benefits, Medicaid, TANF, AFDC, etc.). If any member of your immediate family has received such relief or assistance, please give full details including identity of person(s) receiving relief or assistance, dates for which relief or assistance was received, place, and total amount received during this time:

45) Please give the requested information about your parents, brothers, sisters, aunts, uncles, and grandparents, living or deceased. As to residence, show street address, city, and state, if in the United States; otherwise show only country:

Name: (Last, First, Middle) Alien Registration Number:	Citizen of What Country: Birth Date: (Month, Day, Year)	Relationship to Me: Birth Date: (City and Country)	Immigration Status of Listed Relative
███████████ A#: ███████████	Philippines 06/28/1952	Father Mauban Philippines	LPR
Complete Address of Current Residence, if Living: _____ ██████████████████			
███████████ A#: N/A	USA 03/12/1956	Mother Mauban Philippines	USA
Complete Address of Current Residence, if Living: _____ ██████████████████			

PART 7 - MISCELLANEOUS INFORMATION *(Continued on page 6)*

46) I ☐ - have ☒ - have not entered the United States as a crewman after June 30, 1964.

47) I ☐ - have ☒ - have not been admitted as, or after arrival in the United States acquired the status of, an exchange alien.

48) I ☒ - have ☐ - have not submitted address reports as required by section 265 of the Immigration and Nationality Act.

49) I ☒ - have ☐ - have never (either in the United States or in any foreign country) been arrested, summoned into court as a defendant, convicted, fined, imprisoned, placed on probation, or forfeited collateral for an act involving a felony, misdemeanor, or breach of any public law or ordinance (including, but not limited to, traffic violations or driving incidents involving alcohol). *(If answer is in the affirmative, please give a brief description of each offense including the name and location of the offense, date of conviction, any penalty imposed, any sentence imposed, and the time actually served.)*

07/24/2007 - misdemeanor credit/debit card fraud in violation of section 484E(d) of the California Penal Code. 36 months probation, 3 days jail.

12/29/2008 - felony possession of a controlled substance in violation of section 11337(a) of the California Health and Safety Code. 24 months probation, 2 days jail.

12/29/2008 - felony possession of a controlled substance in violation of section 11337(a) of the California Health and Safety Code. 24 months probation, 1 day jail.

50) Have you ever served in the Armed Forces of the United States? ☐ - Yes ☒ - No. If "Yes" please state branch *(Army, Navy, etc.)* and service number: _____

Place of entry on duty: *(City and State)* _____

Date of entry on duty: *(Month, Day, Year)* _____   Date of discharge: *(Month, Day, Year)* _____

Type of discharge: *(Honorable, Dishonorable, etc.)* _____

I served in active duty status from: *(Month, Day, Year)* _____ to *(Month, Day, Year)* _____

51) Have you ever left the United States or the jurisdiction of the district where you registered for the draft to avoid being drafted into the military or naval forces of the United States?   ☐ Yes ☒ No

52) Have you ever deserted from the military or naval forces of the United States while the United States was at war?   ☐ Yes ☒ No

53) If male, did you register under the Military Selective Service Act or any applicable previous Selective Service (Draft) Laws?   ☐ Yes ☐ No
If "Yes," please give date, Selective Service number, local draft board number, and your last draft classification: _____

54) Were you ever exempted from service because of conscientious objection, alienage, or any other reason?   ☐ Yes ☒ No

55) Please list your present or past membership in or affiliation with every political organization, association, fund, foundation, party, club, society, or similar group in the United States or any other place since your 16th birthday. Include any foreign military service in this part. If none, write "None." Include the name of the organization, location, nature of the organization, and the dates of membership.

Name of Organization	Location of Organization	Nature of Organization	Member From: *(Month, Day, Year)*	Member To: *(Month, Day, Year)*

PART 7 - MISCELLANEOUS INFORMATION (Continued)

56) Have you ever:

☐ Yes ☒ No been ordered deported, excluded, or removed?

☐ Yes ☒ No overstayed a grant of voluntary departure from an Immigration Judge or the Department of Homeland Security (DHS), formerly the Immigration and Naturalization Service (INS)?

☐ Yes ☒ No failed to appear for deportation or removal?

57) Have you ever been:

☐ Yes ☒ No a habitual drunkard?

☐ Yes ☒ No one whose income is derived principally from illegal gambling?

☐ Yes ☒ No one who has given false testimony for the purpose of obtaining immigration benefits?

☐ Yes ☒ No one who has engaged in prostitution or unlawful commercialized vice?

☐ Yes ☒ No involved in a serious criminal offense and asserted immunity from prosecution?

☐ Yes ☒ No a polygamist?

☐ Yes ☒ No one who brought in or attempted to bring in another to the United States illegally?

☐ Yes ☒ No a trafficker of a controlled substance, or a knowing assister, abettor, conspirator, or colluder with others in any such controlled substance offense (not including a single offense of simple possession of 30 grams or less of marijuana)?

☐ Yes ☒ No inadmissible or deportable on security-related grounds under sections 212(a)(3) or 237(a)(4) of the INA?

☐ Yes ☒ No one who has ordered, incited, assisted, or otherwise participated in the persecution of an individual on account of his or her race, religion, nationality, membership in a particular social group, or political opinion?

☐ Yes ☒ No a person previously granted relief under sections 212(c) or 244(a) of the INA or whose removal has previously been cancelled under section 240A of the INA?

If you answered "Yes" to any of the above questions, explain:

58) The following certificates or other supporting documents are attached hereto as a part of this application: (*Refer to the Instructions for*

See Attached

PART 8 - SIGNATURE OF PERSON PREPARING FORM, IF OTHER THAN APPLICANT

(Read the following information and sign below)

I declare that I have prepared this application at the request of the person named in Part 1, that the responses provided are based on all information of which I have knowledge, or which was provided to me by the applicant, and that the completed application was read to the applicant in a language the applicant speaks fluently for verification before he or she signed the application in my presence. I am aware that the knowing placement of false information on the Form EOIR-42A may subject me to civil penalties under 8 U.S.C. 1324c.

Signature of Preparer:	Print Name:	Date:
	Christopher A. Reed	08/28/2014
Daytime Telephone #:	Address of Preparer: *(Number and Street, City, State, Zip Code)*	
(562) 495-0554	Law Offices of Brian D. Lerner, APC 3233 E. Broadway Long Beach, CA 90803	

PART 9 - SIGNATURE

APPLICATION NOT TO BE SIGNED BELOW UNTIL APPLICANT APPEARS BEFORE AN IMMIGRATION JUDGE

I swear or affirm that I know the contents of this application that I am signing, including the attached documents and supplements, and that they are all true to the best of my knowledge, taking into account the correction(s) numbered _____ to _____, if any, that were made by me or at my request.

_____

(Signature of Applicant or Parent or Guardian)

Subscribed and sworn to before me by the above named applicant at _____

_____

Immigration Judge

_____

Date: (Month, Day, Year)

PART 10 - PROOF OF SERVICE

I hereby certify that a copy of the foregoing Form EOIR-42A was: ☐ - delivered in person ☐ - mailed first class, postage prepaid

on _____ to the Assistant Chief Counsel for the DHS (U.S. Immigration and Customs Enforcement-ICE)
(Month, Day, Year)

at _____
(Number and Street, City, State, Zip Code)

_____

Signature of Applicant (or Attorney or Representative)

Addendum

Part 3. 23) Additional Departure/Arrival History:

Port of Departure: LAX
Departure Date: 1994
Purpose of Travel: Vacation
Destination: Philippines
Port of Return: LAX
Return Date: 1994
Inspected and Admitted?: Yes

Part 6. 45) Additional Relatives:

████████████████████████

Citizenship: Philippines
DOB: 09/25/1975
Place and Country of Birth: Mauban, Philippines
████████████████████████

Immigration Status: LPR

████████████████████████

Citizenship: USA
DOB: 10/29/1981
Place and Country of Birth: Mauban, Philippines
████████████████████████

Immigration Status: USC

Department of Homeland Security
U.S. Citizenship and Immigration Service.

Form I-797C, Notice of Action

THIS NOTICE DOES NOT GRANT ANY IMMIGRATION STATUS OR BENEFIT.

RECEIPT NUMBER		CASE TYPE	EOIR 42A Application for Cancellation of Removal
SRC-14-237-50478			for Certain Permanent Residents

RECEIVED DATE	PRIORITY DATE	APPLICANT
SEPTEMBER 03, 2014		▇▇▇▇▇▇▇▇▇▇

NOTICE DATE	PAGE	PRINCIPAL ALIEN
SEPTEMBER 5, 2014	1 of 1	

CHRISTOPHER REED
LAW OFFICES OF BRIAN D LERNER
3233 E BROADWAY
LONG BEACH CA 90803

Notice Type: Receipt Notice
Amount received: $100.00

This notice acknowledges the above receipt of your designated application and fee
as part of the requirements before the immigration judge can grant relief in your case.

The above application has been received and accepted as an I-485 receipt at the Texas Service Center.
The actual case you submitted is listed in the block marked 'CASE TYPE'

Please notify us immediately if any of the above information is incorrect.

A fingerprint appointment will be scheduled and you will be notified at a later date.

Always remember to call customer service if you move while your case is pending.

You will be notified separately about any other cases you have filed.

CITIZENSHIP & IMMIGRATION SERVICE
TEXAS SERVICE CENTER
P O BOX 851488 - DEPT A
MESQUITE, TX 751851488
Customer Service Telephone: (800) 375-5283

EXHIBITS

EXHIBIT '1'

Respondent's Certificate of Live Birth

Municipal Form No. 102 (Revised Dec. 1, 1955)

REPUBLIC OF THE PHILIPPINES

(TO BE ACCOMPLISHED IN QUADRUPLICATE)

CERTIFICATE OF LIVE BIRTH

(FILL OUT COMPLETELY, ACCURATELY, LEGIBLY IN INK OR TYPEWRITER)

Register Number:

(a) Civil Registrar-General No.

(b) Local Civil Registrar No.

Province: **Quezon**

City or Municipality: **Mauban**

1. PLACE OF BIRTH

a. PROVINCE **Quezon**

b. CITY OR MUNICIPALITY **Mauban**

c. NAME OF HOSPITAL OR INSTITUTION (If not in hospital, give street address):

d. IS PLACE OF BIRTH INSIDE CITY LIMITS?   Yes ☐   No ☐

2. USUAL RESIDENCE OF MOTHER (Where does mother live?)

a. PROVINCE **Quezon**

b. CITY OR MUNICIPALITY **Mauban**

c. NUMBER AND STREET **32 Lluspa St.**

d. IS RESIDENCE INSIDE CITY LIMITS?   Yes ☐   No ☐

e. IS RESIDENCE ON A FARM?   Yes ☐   No ☐

3. NAME (Type or print)   First ████████   Middle ████   Last ████

4. SEX **F**   5a. THIS BIRTH   Single ☒   Twin ☐   Triplet ☐

5b. IF TWIN OR TRIPLET, WAS CHILD   1st ☐   2nd ☐   3rd ☐

6. DATE OF BIRTH   Month **Jan.**   Day **26**   Year **1979**

FATHER

7. NAME   First **Horacio**   Middle **Villamayor**   Last **Uriazo**

Religion **Catholic**   8. NATIONALITY **Filipino**   8a. RACE **Brown**

9. AGE (At time of this birth)   Years **27**

10. BIRTHPLACE **Mauban, Quezon**

11a. USUAL OCCUPATION **Laborer**   11b. KIND OF BUSINESS OR INDUSTRY

MOTHER

12. MAIDEN NAME   First **Solita**   Middle **de los Santos**   Last **Estaya**

Religion **Catholic**   13. NATIONALITY **Filipino**   13a. RACE **Brown**

14. AGE (At time of this birth)   Years **23**

15. BIRTHPLACE **Mauban, Quezon**

16. CHILDREN PREVIOUSLY BORN TO MOTHER (Do not include this birth)

a. How many children are now living? **1**

b. How many other children were born alive but are now dead? **0**

c. How many fetal deaths (fetuses born dead any time after conception)? **0**

17a. INFORMANT'S SIGNATURE

b. NAME IN PRINT: ████████

c. ADDRESS:

18. MOTHER'S MAILING ADDRESS: (Number, Street, City or Municipality, Province) **31 Lluspa St., Mauban, Quezon**

19. **ATTENDANT AT BIRTH**

I hereby certify that I attended the birth of this child who was born alive at **2:00** o'clock **A.** M. on the date above indicated.

a. SIGNATURE

b. NAME IN PRINT: **SOLITA NAVA**

c. ADDRESS: **Mauban, Quezon**

d. DATE SIGNED BY ATTENDANT AT BIRTH:

e. TITLE OF ATTENDANT AT BIRTH: ☐ M. D.   ☐ MIDWIFE   ☐ NURSE   ☒ OTHERS (Specify) **Hilot**

20. RECEIVED IN THIS OFFICE BY:

a. SIGNATURE

b. NAME IN PRINT: **PABLO A. de SILVA**

c. TITLE OR POSITION: **Local Civil Registrar**

d. DATE:

21. a. GIVEN NAME ADDED FROM SUPPLEMENTAL REPORT:

b. DATE WHEN GIVEN NAME WAS SUPPLIED:

22a. LENGTH OF PREGNANCY   COMPLETED WEEKS

22b. WEIGHT AT BIRTH   Lbs.   Oz.

23. LEGITIMATE   ☒ Yes   ☐ No

24. DATE AND PLACE OF MARRIAGE OF PARENTS (For legitimate birth)

July (Month)   **25** (Date)   **1975** (Year)

City or Municipality **Lucena**   Province **City**

25. THIS CERTIFICATE IS PREPARED BY:

SIGNATURE

NAME IN PRINT: **IRMINA G. VELASCO**

TITLE OR POSITION: **City Reg., R. Custodian, Vaca Clerk**

DATE:

(SPACE FOR MEDICAL AND HEALTH ITEMS FOR SPECIAL PURPOSES)

Republic of the Philippines
Municipality of Mauban
Quezon
OFFICE OF THE LOCAL CIVIL REGISTRAR

TO WHOM IT MAY CONCERN:

This is to certify that according to the records on file in this office the following is the records of birth of one; ████████████████, to wit:

Name of Child - - - - - - - - - -
Date of Birth - - - - - - - - -
Name of Father - - - - - - - -
Nationality - - - - - - - - - -
Name of Mother - - - - - - - -
Nationality - - - - - - - - - -
Legitimate - - - - - - - - -
Nationality - - - - - - - - -
Register of Birth - - - - - -
P a g e - - - - - - - - - - - -
Line No. - - - - - - - - - -
Book No. - - - - - - - - - -   XV- Chronological Order

Issued this 14th day of ___January___, 19 83 at

Mauban, Quezon

Paid Under O.R. No. 9843274
Date January 14, _____, 19 83
Amount ₱   3.00

rolly/1/8/83

PABLO A. de SILVA
Local Civil Registrar

BY: _____
JESUS C. FOLLANTE
Asst. Local Civil Registrar
& Asst. Municipal Treasurer

EXHIBIT '2'

Respondent's Certificate of Baptism

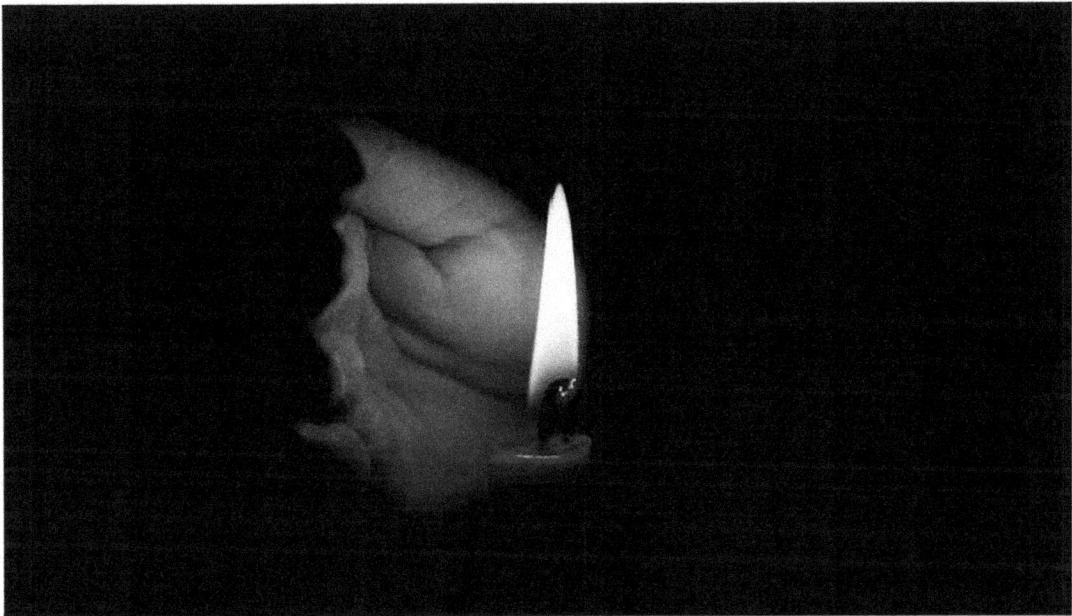

Certificate of Baptism

DIOCESE OF LUCENA
Parish of St. Bonaventure
Mauban, Quezon

THIS IS TO CERTIFY

That .... ██████████ ....

Child of .. ██████████ ....

and ....

born in MAUBAN, QUEZON .... on the

.... 26th day of JANUARY ...., 19 79.. was solemnly BAPTIZED

on the .... 19th day of AUGUST ...., 1979..

ACCORDING TO THE RITE OF THE
ROMAN CATHOLIC CHURCH

by the Rev. FR. BENJAMIN L. RODA JR. ....

the Sponsors being ██████████ ....

and .... ██████████ ....

the Baptismal Register No. .... 42 Page 40 Line 8

of this Church.

Dated October 23 ...., 19 84.

Purpose: .... for reference

REV. FR. DOMINGO B. EDORA
PARISH PRIEST

by: _Parish sec_

EXHIBIT '3'

Respondent's I-94, Social Security Card and Passport

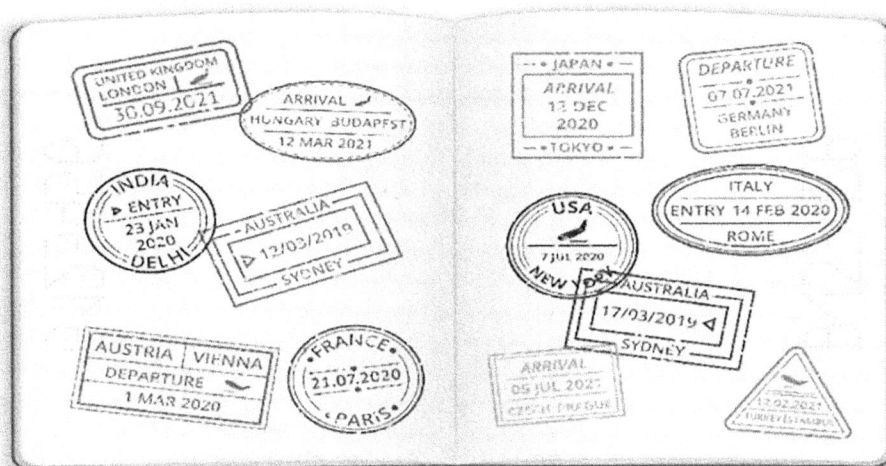

...on work... ...nt, serves as
...porary I-551 evidencing
...nt residency.

Date 08 Aug 2012 C
Officer LAX0270 B
PLOYMENT AUTHORIZED P
Until 09 Aug 2013

C27023

Family Name

First (Given) Name

3. Birth Date (Day/Mo/Yr)
2 6 | 10 | 17 | 9

4. Country of Citizenship
PHILIPPINES

5. Sex (Male or Female)
FEMALE

5. Passport Number

7. Airline and Flight Number

8. Country Where You Live
USA

9. City Where You Boarded

10. City Where Visa Was Issued

11. Date Issued (Day/Mo/Yr)

12. Address While in the United States (Number and Street)

13. City and State
LOS ANGELES, CA 90026

VALID FOR WORK ONLY
WITH INS AUTHORIZATION
SOCIAL SECURITY

MGA PAGTATAKDA-LIMITATIONS

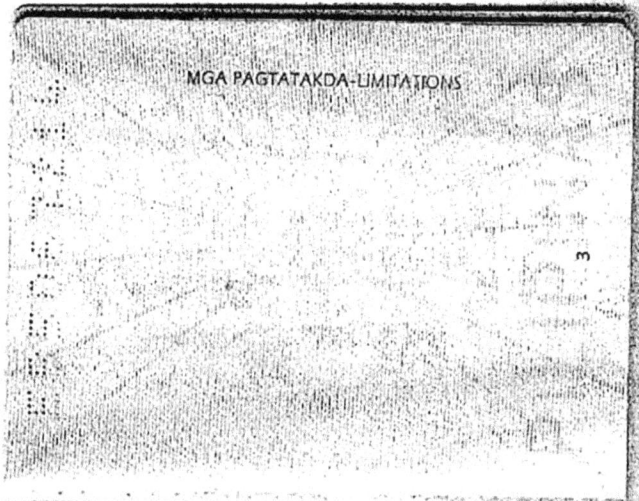

REPUBLIKA NG PILIPINAS / REPUBLIC OF THE PHILIPPINES
PASAPORTE
PASSPORT

P PHL EB5087214

26 Jan 90 FILIPINO
F MAUBAN QUEZON
02 Apr 12 PCG LOS ANGELES
01 Apr 17

EXHIBIT '4'

Respondent's School Records

Fresno Unified
School District

Consideration of Deferred Action for Childhood Arrivals

Record of Enrollment

Date	MARCH 25, 2014
Current **Last** Name	
Current **First** Name	
Current **Middle** Initial	
Student **Last** Name (at time of attendance)	
Student **First** Name (at time of attendance)	
Student **Middle** Initial (at time of attendance)	
Student DOB	
Address, City, State, Zip Code (of record)	
Date of District Enrollment	9/7/1994
Years of Enrollment	4

Status of District Enrollment

CURRENT   Current Student ◯ Yes   ◉ No

Current School	
School Address	
Current Grade Level	
Name of Program (i.e. ESL, GED, Job Training)	

GRADUATE   Graduate ◯ Yes   ◉ No

Graduation Month/Year	
High School Attended	
School Address	
Name of Program (i.e. ESL, GED, Job Training)	

GED   GED Completion ◯ Yes   ◉ No

School Attended	
School Address	
GED Completion Month/Year	

Ambra D. Dorsey, J.D.
Custodian of Records

Fresno Unified School District, Student Records Office   1350 M Street, Fresno, CA 93721   (559) 457-3362

MANDATORY PERMANENT RECORD
(CUMULATIVE FOLDER) ELEMENTARY

333D/81 | 01-26-79 FB
SCHOOL 13
STUDENT IDENTIFIED AS IEP
GRADE: 04

Place of Birth ___ Philippines ___ FB
(City) (State)

Date of Birth 1-26-79

How Verified
Birth Certificate ☐ Baptismal Record ☐ Affidavit ☐ Sex F T-Twin ☐ Blank-No ☐ Grades repeated: ☐

Date Entered	School	Home Address	Zip Code	Phone	Trans. to	Date	Sent to
9/5/89	Del Mar		93704				
5-9-92	Pyle		93726			3/6/92	
						6-92	

TRANSCRIPT REC

Legal Name _____ (Use Pencil)

Grade and Room Number
Pre Sch	K	1	2	3
			8	
		4	3	8

ADULT CODE 1   LANG OF HOME 3   ETHNIC CODE 6   SPEC. ED. CODE   HEALTH CODE

Child Lives With (Use Pencil) _____ Date 9/5/89

CHDP Complete: _____ Date _____

FATHER
Name _____ (Last) _____ (First) _____ (Middle)
Address _____ SAME AS STUDENT _____ (City) (State)
Occupation Benefit Approver _____ (State or Country of Birth) Philippines (Citizenship) US ☐ Other ☑

MOTHER
Name _____ (Last) _____ (First) Estaya (Middle)
Address _____ SAME AS STUDENT _____ (City) (State)
Occupation Benefit Approver _____ (State or Country of Birth) Phillipines (Citizenship) US ☑ Other ☐

STEPFATHER STEPMOTHER, GUARDIAN OR FOSTER PARENTS
Name _____ (Last) _____ (First) _____ (Middle)
Address _____ (City) (State)
Occupation _____ (State or Country of Birth) _____ (Citizenship) US ☐ Other ☐

List all other children in the household.
		Year of Birth				Year of Birth
1.	Edmund	75	7.		
2.	Allysa	85	8.		
3.			9.		

(CUMULATIVE FOLDER) ELEMENTARY

SCHOOL: 13
GRADE: 04
STUDENT IDENTIFIED AS LEP
PRIMARY LANGUAGE: TAGALOG
DATE: 09/27/89

RECORDING REPORT CARDS

Record all grades in permanent black ink.
Column a -- Partial grades
Column b -- Final grades

If achievement and effort marks are given,
record only achievement marks. If effort
only is graded, enter the effort mark.

ACHIEVEMENT
A - Superior
B - Above Average
C - Average
D - Fulfillment of minimum req.
F - Failure to meet minimum req.
X - Not graded this period

EFFORT / MARKS
G - Good
S - Satisfactory
N - Needs to Improve

	Pre School	1st yr.	2nd yr.	3rd yr.	4th yr.	5th yr.	6th yr.	7th yr.	8th yr.
Teacher						Leno	Phieu		
Grade						4	5		
School						Bal Mad	Balmas		
Year in School									
School Year	19__ 19__	19__ 19__	19__ 19__	19__ 19__	19__ 19__	19__ 19__	19__ 19__	19__ 19__	19__ 19__
Days Enrolled						E180 -A180	E18C .A176	E180 A171	
Days Attended									

Subjects:
Reading
Mathematics
English Oral Language
         Written Language
Handwriting
Spelling
Social Science
Health/Science
Physical Education
Art
Music
Instrumental Music Band
                    Orchestra
Citizenship
Attendance in Summer School

K-Preschool

1

PHOTO RECORD
Primary | Intermed

PHOTO | PHOT

D.P.T.	MEASLES	POLIO	PREVIOUS SCHOOL ON ORIGINAL J.H.S. ENTRY	

	FATHER	MOTHER	GUARDIAN
NAME	▮		
BIRTHPLACE	Phillipines	PHILLIPINES	
OCCUPATION	Farmworker	Benefit Approver	

DATE ENTER	SCHOOL	HOME ADDRESS	JUNIOR HIGH ATTENDANC▮
9/8/92	Ft. Miller	▮	GRADE EXCUSED UNEXCU▮
			07 E- 7 U-
			08 E- 6 U- 2

DATE	TRANSFERRED TO	DATE	TRANSCRIPTS SENT TO
JUN 16 1994	McLANE HIGH SCHOOL		

07

COURSE TITLE 07	GRADE	EFFORT	ATTITUDE	STUDY HABITS
LANG 7B	A	G	G	G
GEOG 7B	A	G	G	G
EXPLO 7	C	S	S	S
MATH 7B	C	N	S	S
HLTH/L.S. 7B	B	G	G	S
COED P.E.	B	G	G	S
HMRM 7B			S	S
71 11/06/92				

COURSE TITLE 07	GRADE	EFFORT	ATTITUDE	STUDY HABITS
LANG 7B	A	S	S	S
GEOG 7B	B	N	S	S
EXPLO 7	B	S	S	S
MATH 7B	F	N	N	N
HLTH/L.S. 7B	C	N	S	S
COED P.E.	B	N	N	S
HMRM 7B		G	S	S
71 01/29/93				

COURSE TITLE 07	GRADE	EFFORT	ATTITUDE	STUDY HABITS
LANG 7B	B	S	S	S
WRLD HIST 7B	B	S	N	S
HLTH/L.S. 7B	A	S	S	S
PEER COUNS	A	G	G	G
MATH 7B	C	S	S	S
COED P.E.	C	S	S	S
HMRM 7B		G		S
71 04/02/93				

COURSE TITLE 07	GRADE	EFFORT	ATTITUDE	STUDY HABITS
LANG 7B	B	N	S	N
WRLD HIST 7B	C	N	N	N
MATH 7B	D	S	S	S
PEER COUNS	B	S	S	S
HLTH/L.S. 7B	B	S	N	N
COED P.E.	C	S		S
HMRM 7B		S	G	
71 06/17/93				

9TH GRADE

COURSE TITLE 08	GRADE	EFFORT	ATTITUDE	STUDY HABITS
LANG 8B	B	S	G	S
U.S. HIST 8B	F	N	S	N
SCI 8B	D	S	S	S
COED PE	B	G	G	S
MATH 8B	C	S	G	G
LASER LAB	A	S	S	S
HR8B/7:55AM		S	G	
71 11/05/93				

COURSE TITLE 08	GRADE	EFFORT	ATTITUDE	STUDY HABITS
LANG 8B	C	S	S	S
U.S. HIST 8B	C	G	N	S
SCI 8B	D	N	E	S
COED PE	B	G	S	G
MANUFCTRNG 8	E	N	N	N
MATH 8B	D	N	S	S
LASER LAB	A	N	A	S
HR8B/7:55AM		S		
71 01/28/94				

COURSE TITLE 08	GRADE	EFFORT	ATTITUDE	STUDY HABITS
LANG 8B	F	N	N	N
U.S. HIST 8B	D	S	S	S
SCI 8B	D	S	S	S
COED PE	F	N	N	N
ART	C	N	N	S
MATH 8B	D	S	S	S
HR8B/7:55AM		S	S	
71 04/15/94				

8TH GRADE CONSTITUTION TEST FAILED

COURSE TITLE 08	GRADE	EFFORT	ATTITUDE	STUDY HABITS
LANG 8B	F	N	S	N
U.S. HIST 8B	F	N	N	N
SCI 8B	D	N	N	S
COED PE	F	N	S	N
ART	F	S	S	S
MATH 8B	D	N	N	N
HR8B/7:55AM		N		S
71 06/16/94				

Name

Name _____   Rm. 8   Grade 4   School _Del Mar_

Principal _Mr. Alexander_   Teacher _Mrs. Lipea_   School Year 19 89 - 19 90

EXPLANATION OF TERMS

ACHIEVEMENT:
The quality of accomplishment compared to the expectations for his/her grade level.

EFFORT:
The teacher's assessment of how the student applies himself/herself to the task.

GRADE LEVEL:
Determined by the age designation for the State textbooks and district materials used by the students.

DEFINITION OF MARKS

ACHIEVEMENT	EFFORT
A Superior	G Good
B Above Average	S Satisfactory
C Average	N Needs to
D Fulfillment of minimum req.	Improve
F Failure to meet minimum req.	
X Not graded this period	

	FIRST PERIOD		SECOND PERIOD		THIRD PERIOD		FOURTH PERIOD	
	ACHIEVEMENT	EFFORT	ACHIEVEMENT	EFFORT	ACHIEVEMENT	EFFORT	ACHIEVEMENT	EFFORT
READING	B	G	A	G	A	G	A	G
MATHEMATICS	B	G	B	G	B	G	B	G
ENGLISH Oral Language*	A	G	B	G	B	G	B	G
Written Language	A	G	B	G	B	G	B	G
HANDWRITING	A	G	A	G	A	G	A	G
SPELLING	A	G	A	G	A	G	A	G
SOCIAL STUDIES	B	G	B	G	B	G	B	G
HEALTH / SCIENCE**	B	G	B	G	B	G	B	G
PHYSICAL EDUCATION	C	C	C	C	C	C	C	C
ART	C		C		C		C	
MUSIC								
INSTRUMENTAL MUSIC Band								
Orchestra								

GRADE LEVEL ACHIEVEMENT

	First Quarter				Second Quarter				Third Quarter				Fourth Quarter			
	Above	On	Below		Above	On	Below		Above	On	Below		Above	On	Below	
Rdg																
Math																

CITIZENSHIP	1	2	3	4
Conduct in Class	G	G	S	G
Behavior on Playground	G	G	G	G
Accepts Responsibility	G	G	G	G

ATTENDANCE	1	2	3	4
DAYS ABSENT	0	0	0	0
TIMES TARDY	0	0	0	0
Homework	C	G	G	G

First grade students will be given only effort marks for the 1st report period.

COMMENTS

Quarter 1 _Conference_

SIGNATURE OF TEACHER ☐
Conference Requested ☐

SIGNATURE OF PARENT OR GUARDIAN ☐
Conference Requested ☐

Tear off and return to school.

Quarter 2 _Carried on an interesting and too good parent conf. ..._

SIGNATURE OF TEACHER ☐
Conference Requested ☐

SIGNATURE OF PARENT OR GUARDIAN ☐
Conference Requested ☐

Tear off and return to school.

Quarter 3 _Very bright ..._

SIGNATURE OF PARENT OR GUARDIAN ☐
Conference Requested ☐

SIGNATURE OF TEACHER ☐
Conference Requested ☐

Tear off and return to school.

Quarter 4 _What an outstanding girl ..._

SIGNATURE OF PARENT OR GUARDIAN ☐
Conference Requested ☐

FRESNO UNIFIED SCHOOL DISTRICT - FRESNO, CALIFORNIA - PERMANENT RECORD FORM   CLASS OF 1999   PRINTED: 3/01/00 11:47 AM   PAGE: 2
** HIGH SCHOOL RECORD **

FRESNO,   CA 93722

ID#: 333081   BIRTH: 1/26/79   SEX: F   FATHER: GUARDIAN:
GR: 10   BDATE VERIFIED: AFFIDAVIT   HORACIO
LEGAL NAME: CURRENT SCHOOL: RESTART/TCW   MOTHER: SOLITA

SSN: 607-22-1783   BPLACE: FB

```
GRADE CODES:
A-EXCEPTIONAL          CITIZENSHIP:
B-ABOVE AVERAGE        S-SATISFACTORY
C-AVERAGE              P-POOR
D-BELOW AVERAGE        U-UNSATISFACTORY
P-PASS
E-EXCUSED             COURSE LEVEL:
F-FAILURE            AP-ADVANC PLCMNT
I-INCOMPLETE          B-BILINGUAL
N-NO GRADE/NO CREDIT  G-GATE
W-WITHDRAW/NO PENALTY H-HONORS
WF-WITHDRAW/FAIL      I-ENG IMMERSION
FA-FAIL/ATTENDANCE    P-COLLEGE PREP
                     S-SDAIE
                     SDC-SP DAY CLASS
```

GRADUATION REQUIREMENTS

SUBJECT	CREDIT REQUIRED	CREDIT COMPLETED	CREDIT NEEDED
ENGLISH LANGUAGE ARTS	30.0	10.0	20.0
AMERICAN GOVERNMENT	5.0	.0	5.0
U. S. HISTORY	10.0	6.0	4.0
MODERN WORLD HISTORY	10.0	10.0	.0
BIOLOGICAL SCIENCE	10.0	10.0	.0
PHYSICAL SCIENCE	10.0	10.0	.0
MATHEMATICS	20.0	10.0	10.0
PHYSICAL EDUCATION	30.0	15.0	15.0
SOCIOLOGY FOR LIVING	10.0	10.0	.0
FOREIGN LANGUAGE/ART	10.0	10.0	.0
ECONOMICS	5.0	.0	5.0
ELECTIVES	75.0	15.0	60.0
TOTAL	225.0	106.0	119.0

IMMUNIZATIONS --
POLIO   06/27/89 06/11/89 02/28/9
DTP   06/27/89 08/11/89 02/28/S
MEASLES   06/27/89
MUMPS   06/27/89
RUBELLA   06/27/89
TB SKIN   08/03/89   RESULT: 15
CHEST X   08/03/89   RESULT: N

STATE REQUIRED PROFICIENCY (BSA)
READING: PASS   MATH: FAIL
WRITING: PASS   SAMPLE: NT

GRADE POINT AVERAGES:

NON-AUGMENTED (10-12) 2.105
ELIGIBILITY (PER)   2.130

RANK: 178 CLASS SIZE: 429
GRADUATION DATE: NON GRADUATE
SEMESTERS CSF:

COURSE NAME	GR	CRED EARN	C T	C D
9TH 94/95-02				
**BULLARD HIGH	F	.0	S	
KEYBRD/TYP +	F	.0	S	
ENGLISH IA P	F	.0	P	
MATH A 1SEM	F	.0	S	
AUTO MECH I+	F	.0	S	
OFFICE SERV	B	5.0	S	
ACADEMIC GPA	.000			
10TH 95/96-04				
**PHILLIPPINES	N	.0	S	
CHRISTIAN LIVG	N	.0	S	
FILIPINO	B	10.0	S	
SOC STDIES I/II	B	5.0	S	
SOC STDIES I/II	C	5.0	S	
P E	N	10.0	S	
CHRISTIAN MORAL	C	10.0	S	
ENGLISH	C	10.0	S	
SCI. (BIOLOGY)	C	10.0	S	
MATH (ALG. I)	C	10.0	S	
HOME EC	C	10.0	S	
ACADEMIC GPA	2.250			
10TH 96/97-02				
**RESTART/TCW	D	6.0	S	
US HISTORY P				

COURSE NAME	GR	CRED EARN	C T	C D
PE/IND STUDY	C	3.5	S	
PHYS SCI P	C	.0	S	
ACADEMIC GPA	1.625			
10TH 96/97-04				
**RESTART/TCW	N	.0	S	
ENGLISH II	B	1.5	S	
PE/IND STUDY	N	.0	S	
MATH A	N	.0	S	
US HISTORY P	C	10.0	S	
SOC LIV				
ACADEMIC GPA	2.000			

COURSE NAME	GR	CRED EARN	C T	C D

COURSE NAME	GR	CRED EARN	C T	C D

OFFICIAL TRANSCRIPT SIGNED AND
SEALED BY: S. RICHARDSON

CD: R=REPEATED CLASS, W=WAIVED CLASS, E=EXIT GRADE

FRESNO UNIFIED SCHOOL DISTRICT - FRESNO, CALIFORNIA - PERMANENT RECORD FORM   CLASS OF 1999   PRINTED: 3/01/00 11:47 AM   PAGE: 4
** HIGH SCHOOL RECORD **

ID#: 333081   BIRTH: 1/26/79   SEX: F | FATHER: | GUARDIAN:
GR: 10   BDATE VERIFIED: AFFIDAVIT | HORACIO |
LEGAL NAME: | CURRENT SCHOOL: RESTART/TCW   SSN: 607-22-1783   BPLACE: FB

FRESNO,   CA 93722 | MOTHER:
                                        | SOLITA

ATTENDANCE   GRADE   0   1   2   3   4   5   6   7   8   9   10 11 12

EXCUSED   6   1   48 5
UNEXCUSED   2   48 51

STUDENT ADDRESS LOG

TRANSCRIPTS / RECORDS REQUESTED

DATE   SENT TO   UNTIL   ADDRESS
8/11/99   CENTRAL ADULT SCH
5/21/96   PERSONAL (OFFICIAL)
4/26/95   PHILIPINES
12/08/94 JOHN MARSHALL
12/08/94 H.S. L.A., CA
11/10/94 LOS ANGELES

SCHOOL LOG

D = DROPPED
E = ENROLLED
F = ENTERED FROM
T = TRANSFERRED TO
REASON LEFT:
ADULT EDUCATION
   DATE   SCHOOL   GR
T 5/08/97 ADULT ED   10
D 5/08/97 RESTART/TCW   10
E 9/11/96 RESTART/TCW   10
T 9/10/96 RESTART   11
D 9/10/96 BULLARD HIGH   11
E 8/26/96 BULLARD HIGH   11
T 4/26/95 PHILIPINES   09
D 4/26/95 BULLARD HIGH   09
F 1/04/95 LOS ANGELES
T 10/17/94 UNKNOWN
F 9/07/94 FORT MILLER

FRESNO UNIFIED SCHOOL DISTRICT - FRESNO, CALIFORNIA - PERMANENT RECORD FORM   CLASS OF 1999   PRINTED: 3/01/00 11:47 AM   PAGE: 3
** HIGH SCHOOL RECORD **

ID#: 333081   BIRTH: 1/26/79   SEX: F   FATHER: MOTHER: GUARDIAN:
GR: 10   BDATE VERIFIED: AFFIDAVIT   HORACIO   SOLITA
LEGAL NAME: CURRENT SCHOOL: RESTART/TCW   BPLACE: FB

FRESNO.   CA 93722   SSN: 6

TEST CD DATE   TEST NAME   ------ SCORES ------   TEST CD   DATE   TEST NAME   ------ SCORES ------

                                    T E S T I N G   S C O R E S

BSA   T 08/94 READING   SS:159 PASS
                MATH   SS:129 FAIL
                WRITING SKILLS   SS:156 PASS

ITAS   05 05/91 READING COMPREHENSION   NP:57 NCE:54
                TOTAL READING   NP:42 NCE:46
                TOTAL LANGUAGE   NP:78 NCE:66
                MATH APPLICATION/PROB SLV   NP:28 NCE:38
                TOTAL MATH   NP:30 NCE:39
       06 05/92 READING COMPREHENSION   NP:46 NCE:48
                TOTAL READING   NP:43 NCE:47
                TOTAL LANGUAGE   NP:97 NCE:91
                MATH APPLICATION/PROB SLV   NP:35 NCE:42
                TOTAL MATH   NP:32 NCE:40
       07 05/93 READING COMPREHENSION   NP:32 NCE:40
                TOTAL READING   NP:36 NCE:42
                TOTAL LANGUAGE   NP:57 NCE:54
                MATH APPLICATION/PROB SLV   NP:36 NCE:42
                TOTAL MATH   NP:28 NCE:38
       08 08/94 READING COMPREHENSION   NP:50 NCE:50
                TOTAL READING   NP:46 NCE:48
                TOTAL LANGUAGE   NP:44 NCE:47
                MATH APPLICATION/PROB SLV   NP:23 NCE:35
                TOTAL MATH   NP:09 NCE:22

LPLANG   09/90 OTHER FILIPINO

LPSTAT   08/90 FEP-REDESIG 9/90-8/91

FRESNO UNIFIED SCHOOL DISTRICT - FRESNO, CALIFORNIA - PERMANENT RECORD FORM   CLASS OF 1999   PRINTED: 3/01/00 11:47 AM   PAGE:
** MIDDLE SCHOOL RECORD **

ID#: 333091   BIRTH: 1/26/79   SEX: F
GR: 10   BDATE VERIFIED: AFFIDAVIT
LEGAL NAME:
CURRENT SCHOOL: RESTART/TCW

FATHER: HORACIO
MOTHER: SOLITA
GUARDIAN:
SSN: BPLACE: FB

FRESNO,   CA   93722

MIDDLE SCHOOL GRADE CODES:
A-EXCEPTIONALLY GOOD
B-ABOVE AVERAGE
C-AVERAGE
D-BELOW AVERAGE
P-PASS
E-P.E. MEDICAL EXCUSE
F-FAILURE
WF-WITHDRAWAL WITH F
W-WITHDRAWAL
I-INCOMPLETE

MIDDLE SCHOOL CITIZENSHIP:
G-GOOD
S-SATISFACTORY
N-NEEDS IMPROVEMENT

COURSE TITLE ABBREVIATIONS:
B-BILINGUAL
G-GATE
I-STRUCTURED ENGLISH IMMERSION
P-COLLEGE PREP
S-SDAIE
SDC-SPECIAL DAY CLASS

IMMUNIZATIONS -
POLIO   06/27/89 08/11/89 02/28/9
DTP   06/27/89 08/11/89 02/28/9
MEASLES 06/27/89
MUMPS   06/27/89
RUBELLA 06/27/89
TB SKIN 08/03/89   RESULT: 15
CHEST X 08/03/89   RESULT: N

GRADE POINT AVERAGES:

CUMULATIVE (MID.SCH.) 2.000

STATE REQUIRED PROFICIENCY (ESA)
READING: PASS   MATH: FAIL
WRITING: PASS   SAMPLE: NT

COURSE NAME	GR	CRED EARN	C T	C D
**FORT MILLER MID 7TH 92/93-01				
HMRM 7B				
EXPLO 7	C	5.0	S	
COED P.E.	B	5.0	G	
GEOG 7B	A	5.0	G	
LANG 7B	A	5.0	G	
MATH 7B	B	5.0	G	
HLTH/L.S. 7B	C	5.0	G	
ACADEMIC GPA 3.000				
**FORT MILLER MID 7TH 92/93-02				
HMRM 7B				
EXPLO 7	B	5.0	S	
COED P.E.	B	5.0	N	
GEOG 7B	B	5.0	S	
LANG 7B	B	5.0	S	
MATH 7B	F	.0	S	
HLTH/L.S. 7B	C	5.0	S	
ACADEMIC GPA 2.500				
**FORT MILLER MID 7TH 92/93-03				
HMRM 7B				
PEER COUNS	A	5.0	G	
COED P.E.	C	5.0	S	

COURSE NAME	GR	CRED EARN	C T	C D
**FORT MILLER MID 7TH 92/93-04				
WRLD HIST 7B	B	5.0	N	
LANG 7B	B	5.0	S	
MATH 7B	C	5.0	S	
HLTH/L.S. 7B	C	5.0	S	
ACADEMIC GPA 2.667				
**FORT MILLER MID 7TH 92/93-02				
HMRM 7B				
PEER COUNS	B	5.0	S	
COED P.E.	C	.0	N	
WRLD HIST 7B	B	5.0	S	
LANG 7B	B	5.0	S	
MATH 7B	D	5.0	N	
HLTH/L.S. 7B	B	5.0	S	
ACADEMIC GPA 2.333				
**FORT MILLER MID 8TH 93/94-01				
HR8B/7:55AM				
LASER LAB	A	5.0	S	
COED PE	B	.0	G	
U.S. HIST 8B	F	5.0	G	
LANG 8B	B	5.0	G	
MATH 8B	C	5.0	S	
SCI 8S	D	5.0	S	

COURSE NAME	GR	CRED EARN	C T	C D
ACADEMIC GPA 2.167				
**FORT MILLER MID 8TH 93/94-02				
HR8B/7:55AM				
LASER LAB	A	5.0	N	
MANUFCTRNG	B	5.0	S	
COED PE	B	5.0	G	
U.S. HIST 8B	C	5.0	S	
LANG 8B	D	5.0	S	
MATH 8B	C	5.0	N	
SCI 8B	D	5.0	N	
ACADEMIC GPA 2.167				
**FORT MILLER MID 8TH 93/94-03				
HR8B/7:55AM				
ART	C	5.0	N	
COED PE	O	5.0	S	
U.S. HIST 8B	F	.0	N	
LANG 8B	F	.0	S	
MATH 8B	D	5.0	S	
SCI 8B	D	5.0	S	
ACADEMIC GPA .833				
**FORT MILLER MID 8TH 93/94-04				

COURSE NAME	GR	CRED EARN	C T	C D
HR8B/7:55AM				
ART	D	5.0	S	
COED PE	F	.0	N	
U.S. HIST 8B	F	.0	N	
LANG 8B	F	.0	S	
MATH 8B	D	5.0	N	
SCI 8B	D	5.0	N	
ACADEMIC GPA .333				
**FORT MILLER MID 8TH 93/94-SS				
HIST REV 8	N	.0		
ACADEMIC GPA .000				

CD: R=REPEATED CLASS, W=WAIVED CLASS, E=EXIT GRADE

Name _____ **Grade** 6 YR Track

EXPLANATION OF TERMS

ACHIEVEMENT:
The quality of accomplishment compared to the District standard of expected student achievement for his/her grade level.

EFFORT:
The teacher's assessment of how the student applies himself/herself to the task.

DEFINITION OF MARKS

ACHIEVEMENT
1 Superior
2 Above Average
3 Average
4 Fulfillment of minimum requirements
* Failure to meet minimum requirements
— Not graded this period

EFFORT
G Good
S Satisfactory
N Needs to Improve

		FIRST QUARTER		SECOND QUARTER		THIRD QUARTER		FOURTH QUARTER	
		ACHIEVEMENT	EFFORT	ACHIEVEMENT	EFFORT	ACHIEVEMENT	EFFORT	ACHIEVEMENT	EFFORT
LANGUAGE ARTS	Reading Comprehension	C	S	C	S	C	S	A	G
	Oral Language*	C	S	C	S	C	S	A	G
	Written Language	C	S	C	S	C	S	A	G
	Spelling	B	S	B	S	B	S	A	G
	Handwriting	B	S	B	N	B	N	B	G
MATHEMATICS		D	S	D	N	D	N	B	G
SOCIAL STUDIES		C	S	C	N	C	N	B	G
SCIENCE		B	X	B	X	B	X	X	X
HEALTH		X	X	X	X	X	X	X	X
PHYSICAL EDUCATION		X	N	X	S	X	N	X	G
ART		X	N	X	S	X	N	X	G
MUSIC									
INSTRUMENTAL MUSIC	Band								
	Orchestra								

ENGLISH LANGUAGE PROFICIENCY LEVEL BSM I*
(BSM Levels Range From 1-6)   BSM II****

CITIZENSHIP

		Effort Only
Conduct in Class	N	N	N	G
Behavior on Playground	S	S	N	G
Accepts Responsibility	N	N	N	G

ATTENDANCE

	FIRST	SECOND	THIRD	FOURTH
Days Absent	5	0	2	6
Times Tardy	0	0	N	G

First grade students will have a parent conference for the first grading period, effort races the second grading period, achievement and effort grades for the third and fourth grading periods.

For grades 1-3 only effort marks will be given for all reporting periods.

*Health/Science is marked two grading periods each year.
**For Limited English Students Only. - BSM I for Grades K-2/BSM II for Grades 4-6
— Effort grades only are given in all Language Arts components until child reaches BSM Level 4
— In the other content areas students will receive achievement grades not later

---

Sign, Tear Off and Return to School

COMMENTS

Quarter 1 _____

☐ Check if Conference Requested
SIGNATURE OF TEACHER

Mr. Crassnicklaws

Quarter 2 _____

☐ Check if Conference Requested
SIGNATURE OF PARENT OR GUARDIAN

Sheperd

☐ Check if Conference Requested
SIGNATURE OF TEACHER

Mr. Crassnicklaws

Quarter 3 _____

☐ Check if Conference Requested
SIGNATURE OF PARENT OR GUARDIAN

☐ Check if Conference Requested
SIGNATURE OF TEACHER

☐ Check if Conference Requested
SIGNATURE OF PARENT OR GUARDIAN

☐ Check if Conference Requested
SIGNATURE OF TEACHER

Name _____

Principal **Mrs. Shepard**   Teacher **Mr. Crassnicklaws**   School Year 19 9L - 19 9S

Rm. **29** grade **6** school **Del Mar**

SIGNATURE OF TEACHER

EXHIBIT '5'

Respondent's Alcohol and Drug Counseling Diploma

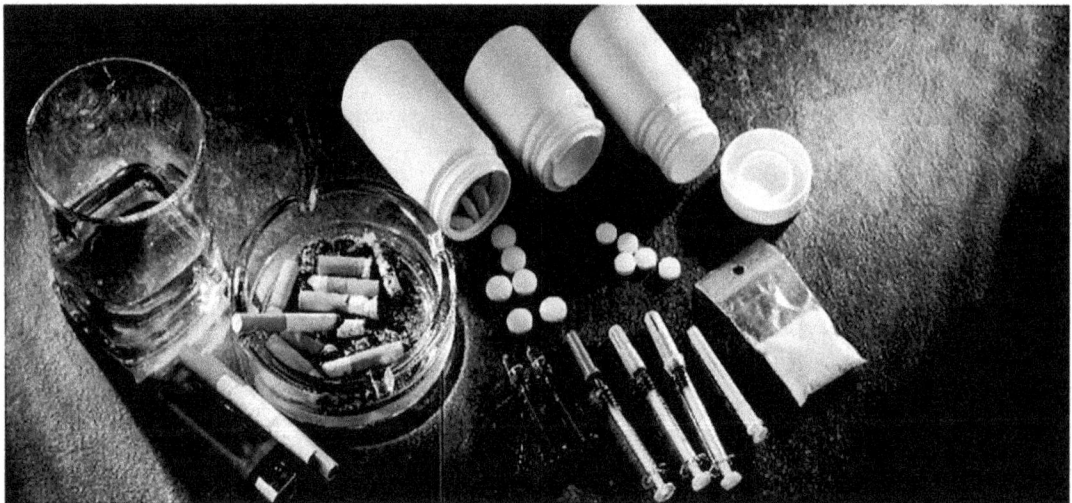

DIPLOMA

PRESENTED TO

Has successfully completed a training course

Alcohol and Drug Counseling

at

ICDC COLLEGE

5422 Sunset Blvd.,
Hollywood, CA 90027

Revikka Gustkher,
Executive Director

11/02/11
Date

Marika Frid,
Campus President, Hollywood Campus

11/02/11
Date

EXHIBIT '6'

Respondent's Parent's U.S. Passports and Permanent Resident Cards

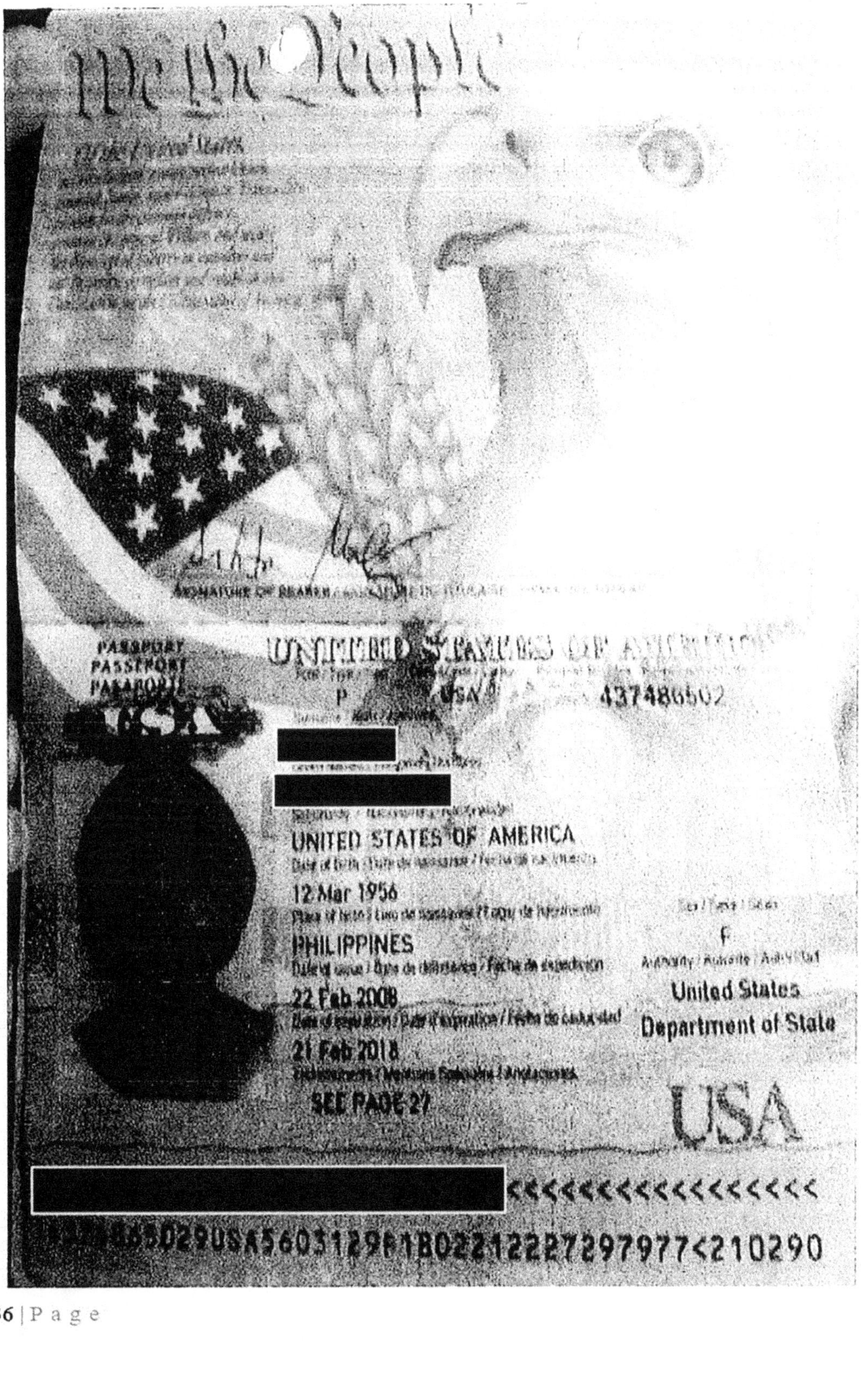

UNITED STATES OF AMERICA

P   USA   437486502

UNITED STATES OF AMERICA

12 Mar 1956

PHILIPPINES

22 Feb 2008

21 Feb 2018

SEE PAGE 27

F

United States
Department of State

USA

<<<<<<<<<<<<<<<

8880290USA5603129M1B0221222727297977<210290

PERMANENT RESIDENT CARD
[redacted]
A# [redacted]
Birthdate Category Sex
M
07/21/19
Resident Since 02/13/85
1USA0391630676MSC0990020094<<
206287M1907210PHL<<<<<<<<<<<4
[redacted]

EXHIBIT '7'

Respondent's Sibling's U.S. Passports and Permanent Resident Cards

LOS-IR2   092575   WAIVED

THE UNITED STATES OF AMERICA

No. 30773772

CERTIFICATE OF NATURALIZATION

USCIS Registration No. A45907649

Personal description of holder as of date of issuance of this Certificate:

I certify that the description given is true, and that the photograph affixed hereto is a likeness of me.

Date of birth: OCTOBER 29, 1981

Sex: MALE

Height: 5 feet 6 inches

Marital status: MARRIED

Country of former nationality: PHILIPPINES

(Complete and true signature of holder)

Be it known that ████████

residing at ████████

having applied to the Director, U.S. Citizenship and Immigration Services, for replacement of a Certificate of Naturalization and having proved to the satisfaction of the Director that s/he

COMPLIED WITH THE APPLICABLE PROVISIONS OF SUCH NATURALIZATION AND WAS ENTITLED TO BE ADMITTED TO CITIZENSHIP; SUCH PERSON HAVING TAKEN THE OATH OF ALLEGIANCE IN A CEREMONY CONDUCTED BY THE U.S. DISTRICT COURT CENTRAL DISTRICT

AT POMONA, CALIFORNIA ON OCTOBER 24, 2007

Now Therefore, in pursuance of the authority contained in Section 343(1) of the Immigration and Nationality Act, this Certificate of Naturalization is issued this 26TH day of NOVEMBER 2013 and the seal of the Department of Homeland Security affixed pursuant to statute.

U.S. Citizenship and Immigration Services

ALTERATION OR MISUSE OF THIS DOCUMENT IS A FEDERAL OFFENSE AND PUNISHABLE BY LAW

1675890

DEPARTMENT OF HOMELAND SECURITY

EXHIBIT '8'

Respondent's ASC Appointment Notice

Department of Homeland Security
U.S. Citizenship and Immigration Servi...

Form I-797C, Notice of Action

THIS NOTICE DOES NOT GRANT ANY IMMIGRATION STATUS OR BENEFIT.

ASC Appointment Notice	APPLICATION/PETITION/REQUEST NUMBER SRC1423750478		NOTICE DATE 09/05/2014
CASE TYPE I485 - APPLICATION TO REGISTER PERMANENT RESIDENCE OR ADJUST STATUS	SOCIAL SECURITY NUMBER	USCIS A# A042049242	CODE 3
ACCOUNT NUMBER	TCR	SERVICE CENTER TSC	PAGE 1 of 1

c/o CHRISTOPHER A REED
LAW OFFICES OF BRIAN D LERNER
3233 E BROADWAY
LONG BEACH CA 90803

To process your application, petition, or request, the U. S. Citizenship & Immigration Services (USCIS) must capture your biometrics.
PLEASE APPEAR AT THE BELOW APPLICATION SUPPORT CENTER AT THE DATE AND TIME SPECIFIED.
IF YOU FAIL TO APPEAR AS SCHEDULED, YOUR APPLICATION, PETITION, OR REQUEST WILL BE CONSIDERED ABANDONED.

APPLICATION SUPPORT CENTER	PLEASE READ THIS ENTIRE NOTICE CAREFULLY.
USCIS WILSHIRE	DATE AND TIME OF APPOINTMENT
1015 WILSHIRE BOULEVARD 1ST FLOOR, SUITE 100	09/23/2014
LOS ANGELES CA 90017	03:00PM

WHEN YOU GO TO THE APPLICATION SUPPORT CENTER TO HAVE YOUR BIOMETRICS TAKEN, YOU MUST BRING:
1. THIS APPOINTMENT NOTICE and
2. PHOTO IDENTIFICATION. Naturalization applicants must bring their Alien Resident Card. All other applicants must bring a passport, driver's license, national ID, military ID, or State-issued photo ID. If you appear without proper identification, you will not be fingerprinted.

CELL PHONES, CAMERAS, OR OTHER RECORDING DEVICES ARE NOT PERMITTED.

REQUEST FOR RESCHEDULING

☐ Please reschedule my appointment. Once USCIS receives your request, you will be sent a new appointment notice. Make a copy of this notice for your records, then mail the original with your request to BFU, Alexandria ASC, Suite 100, 8850 Richmond Hwy, Alexandria, VA 22309-1586

APPLICATION NUMBER
I485 - SRC1423750478

If you have any questions regarding this notice, please call 1-800-375-5283.
WARNING: *Due to limited seating availability in our lobby area, only persons who are necessary to assist with transportation or completing the biometrics worksheet should accompany you. If you have open wounds or bandages/casts when you appear, the USCIS may reschedule your appointment if it is determined your injuries will interfere with taking your biometrics.*

EXHIBIT '9'

Respondent's California Criminal History Information (CALDOJ)

State of California
DEPARTMENT OF JUSTICE

BUREAU OF CRIMINAL INFORMATION AND ANALYSIS
P.O. Box 903417
SACRAMENTO, CA 94203-4170

August 19, 2014

RE: California Criminal History Information

Dear Applicant:

This is in response to your record review request concerning the existence of a California criminal history record maintained in the files of the Department of Justice's Bureau of Criminal Information and Analysis. Your fingerprints did identify to an existing California criminal history record and a copy of that record is enclosed. If you wish to challenge the accuracy or completeness of your record, please complete and return the enclosed form (BCIA 8706) and supporting documentation to the address noted above. As requested, a copy of this record review response has been sent to your designee.

Pursuant to California Penal Code section 11121, the purpose of a record review request is to afford an individual with a copy of their record and to refute any erroneous or inaccurate information contained therein. The intent is not to be used for licensing, certification or employment purposes.

Additionally, California Penal Code sections 11125, 11142, and 11143 does not allow for a person or agency to make a request to another person to provide them with a copy of an individual's criminal history or notification that a record does not exist; does not allow an authorized person to furnish the record to an unauthorized person; nor does it allow an unauthorized person to buy, receive or possess the record or information. A violation of these section codes is a misdemeanor.

Sincerely,

Cindy Santos

Record Review Unit
Applicant Information and Certification Program
Bureau of Criminal Information and Analysis

For KAMALA D. HARRIS
Attorney General

Enclosures
BCIA 8711d (Rev. 08/13)

```
4CMTD782194.IH
RE: QHY.CA0349400.28402571    USR.    DATE:20140819 TIME:  2:25
RESTRICTED-DO NOT USE FOR EMPLOYMENT,LICENSING OR CERTIFICATION PURPOSES
ATTN:APPUSR


*****************************************************************************
FOR CALIFORNIA AGENCIES ONLY - HAS PREVIOUS QUALIFYING OFFENSE.  COLLECT
DNA IF INCARCERATED, CONFINED, OR ON PROBATION OR PAROLE FOLLOWING ANY
MISDEMEANOR OR FELONY CONVICTION.  REQUEST KITS AND INFO AT (510) 620-
3300 OR PC296.PC296@DOJ.CA.GOV.
*****************************************************************************
** PALM PRINT ON FILE AT DOJ FOR ADDITIONAL INFORMATION PLEASE E-MAIL
PALM.PRINT@DOJ.CA.GOV
** III CALIFORNIA ONLY SOURCE RECORD
CII/A28402571
DOB/19790126    SEX/F RAC/HISPANIC
HGT/500  WGT/100  EYE/BRO  HAI/BRO  POB/PI
CTZ/PHILIPPINES
NAM/001 ONLAYAO,ANNA CARISSA

FBI/679551RC6
DMV/B7612926
SOC/607221783
SMT/TAT BACK-UNKNOWN              ; TAT L ANKL-UNKNOWN          ;
     TAT R SHLD-UNKNOWN
* * * *


ARR/DET/CITE:       NAM:001  DOB:19790126
20070602    CAPD FRESNO

CNT:001    #0766634-428787
  470(D) PC-FALSE CHECKS/RECORDS/CERTS/ETC              TOC:F
   SCN:S49A1530023
- - - -
COURT:              NAM:001
20070724  CASC FRESNO CENTRAL

CNT:001    #F107904397
  470(D) PC-FALSE CHECKS/RECORDS/CERTS/ETC              TOC:F
  DISPO:DISMISSED

CNT:002
  530.5(A) PC-GET CREDIT/ETC:USE OTHER'S ID             TOC:F
  DISPO:DISMISSED

CNT:003
  496(A) PC-RECEIVE/ETC KNOWN STOLEN PROPERTY           TOC:F
  DISPO:DISMISSED

CNT:004
  484E(D) PC-USE ACCESS ACCOUNT INFO W/O CONSENT        TOC:F
*DISPO:CONVICTED
   CONV STATUS:MISDEMEANOR PER 17PC
    SEN: 036 MONTHS PROBATION, 003 DAYS JAIL, 003 DAYS JAIL OR FINE,
       FINE, RESTN

  DISPO:CONVICTION CERT BY CLERK OF THE COURT
  DISPO:FOR CERT INFO SEE AUTOMATED ARCHIVE SYS

20081229
  DISPO:EARLY DISMISSAL FROM PROBATION
* * * *

ARR/DET/CITE:       NAM:001  DOB:19790126
```

20080325   CAPD FRESNO   (─)

CNT:001   #0886809-4287b,
  11377(A) HS-POSSESS CONTROLLED SUBSTANCE   TOC:F

CNT:002   TOC:M
  11550(A) HS-USE/UNDER INFL CONTRLD SUBSTANCE
  SCN:S49B0850009
- - - -
COURT: NAM:001
20080514 CASC FRESNO CENTRAL

CNT:001   #F08902017
  11550(A) HS-USE/UNDER INFL CONTRLD SUBSTANCE   TOC:M
  DISPO:DISMISSED

CNT:002   TOC:F
  11377(A) HS-POSSESS CONTROLLED SUBSTANCE
  DISPO:PROC SUSP/DRUG CRT-DEFERRED JUDGEMENT

20081229
  DISPO:DRG CRT/DEFER JDGMNT-TRM CRM PROC REINST
- - - -
COURT: NAM:001
20081229 CASC FRESNO CENTRAL

CNT:001   #F08902017
  11377(A) HS-POSSESS CONTROLLED SUBSTANCE   TOC:F
*DISPO:CONVICTED
  CONV STATUS:FELONY
    SEN: 024 MONTHS PROBATION, 002 DAYS JAIL, WORK PROGRAM, IMP SEN SS

  DISPO:COND OF PROB-DRUG TREATMENT PLACEMENT
* * * *

ARR/DET/CITE: NAM:001 DOB:19790126
20081201   CAPD FRESNO

CNT:001   #08103848-428787
  11377(A) HS-POSSESS CONTROLLED SUBSTANCE   TOC:F

CNT:002   TOC:M
  11364 HS-POSSESS CONTROL SUBSTANCE PARAPHERNA

CNT:003   TOC:F
  12316(B)(1) PC-PROHIBITED OWN/ETC AMMO/ETC
    ADR:20081201 (200,LOMA, ,S,LA,CA,90026)
    SCN:S49B3360019
- - - -
COURT: NAM:001
20081229 CASC FRESNO CENTRAL

CNT:001   #F08907500
  11364 HS-POSSESS CONTROL SUBSTANCE PARAPHERNA
  DISPO:DISMISSED

CNT:002
  11377(A) HS-POSSESS CONTROLLED SUBSTANCE
*DISPO:CONVICTED
  CONV STATUS:FELONY
    SEN: 024 MONTHS PROBATION, 001 DAYS JAIL, WORK PROGRAM, IMP SEN SS

  DISPO:COND OF PROB-DRUG TREATMENT PLACEMENT
  DISPO:CONVICTION CERT BY CLERK OF THE COURT

DISPO:FOR CERT INFO SE(TOMATED ARCHIVE SYS

* * * END MESSAGE * * *

EXHIBIT '10'

Docket Sheet – F07904397

Superior Court of California, County of Fresno

DOCKET REPORT

Case : F07904397 F A

Name : Unlayao, Anna Carissa Estaya

Date of Action	Seq Nbr	Code	Text
06/05/07			
	1	FLDOC	**Original Complaint filed by District Attorney.**
	2	FLNAM	Name filed: ▆▆▆▆▆▆
	3	FLCNT	FELONY charge of 470(d) PC filed as count 1. Date of violation: 06/02/2007.
	4	FLCNT	FELONY charge of 484e(d) PC filed as count 2. Date of violation: 06/02/2007.
	5	FLCNT	FELONY charge of 530.5(a) PC filed as count 3. Date of violation: 06/02/2007.
	6	FLCNT	FELONY charge of 496(a) PC filed as count 4. Date of violation: 06/02/2007.
	7	JLINC	Defendant is in custody at the Fresno County Jail.
	8	BLSET	Court orders bail set in the amount of $47, 000.00.
	9	COJUS	Clerk's office filed JUS8715 form.
06/06/07			
	1	CLADD	**Case calendared on 06/06/07 at 01:30 PM in Department 32, Add-on for Arraignment Initial Appearance.**
	2	HHELD	**Hearing held on 6/6/2007 at 01:30:00 PM in Department 32, Add-on for Arraignment Initial Appearance.**
	3	OFJUD	Judicial Officer: Gottlieb, David, Judge
	4	OFJA	Courtroom Clerk: Gonzales, Tricia
	5	OFREP	Court Reporter: Zoanne Williams
	6	APDDA	People present and are represented by, Ryan McGinthy, Deputy District Attorney.
	7	CLSET2	**Arraignment re: Continued Arraignment set on 06/07/2007 at 08:30 AM in Department 32, Add-on.**
	8	TEXT	Cont. to check custody status
	9	DSCSR	**Defendant remains in custody.**
	10	OFMCD	Minutes of T. Gonzales entered by Delia A on 06/06/2007.
	11	NTJAL	Notice to Sheriff issued.
	12	HHELD	**Hearing held on 6/6/2007 at 01:30:00 PM in Department 32, Add-on for Arraignment Initial Appearance.**
	13	OFJUD	Judicial Officer: ^1^, ^2^
	14	OFJA	Courtroom Clerk: ^1^
	15	OFREP	Court Reporter: ^1^

DOCKET REPORT

Case : F07904397 F A

Name :

Date of Action	Seq Nbr	Code	Text
06/07/07			
	1	FLCRT	Original charging document filed at 1100 Van Ness Avenue^Fresno, CA 93724 USA
	2	HHELD	**Hearing held on 6/7/2007 at 08:30:00 AM in Department 32, Add-on for Arraignment Continued Arraignment.**
	3	OFJUD	Judicial Officer: Gottlieb, David, Judge
	4	OFJA	Courtroom Clerk: Gonzales, Tricia
	5	OFREP	Court Reporter: Williams, Zoanne
	6	APDDA	People present and are represented by, Samuel A Luton, Deputy District Attorney.
	7	JLTXT	**Per deputy, deft. not I/C**
	8	CODFA	Court orders District Attorney to file affidavit in support of arrest warrant.
	9	OFMCD	Minutes of T. Gonzales entered by Delia A on 06/07/2007.
	10	NTJAL	Notice to Sheriff issued.
06/08/07			
	1	TEXT	Surety Bond posted 6/5/07, no Affidavit in support of arrest warrant needed. Deft. to appear 6/18/07 for Arrn.
	2	BBPST	Bail Bond Number LG5-523993 posted in the amount of $2000.00 by ALADDINBB of LGISU.
	3	CLSET2	**Arraignment re: Initial Appearance set on 06/18/2007 at 08:30 AM in Department 32, 3rd Floor.**
06/18/07			
	1	HHELD	**Hearing held on 6/18/2007 at 08:30:00 AM in Department 32, 3rd Floor for Arraignment Initial Appearance.**
	2	OFJUD	Judicial Officer: Gottlieb, David, Judge
	3	OFJA	Courtroom Clerk: Gonzales, Tricia
	4	OFREP	Court Reporter: Gonzales, Valerie
	5	APDDA	People present and are represented by, Ryan McGinthy, Deputy District Attorney.
	6	COCCW	Case having been called at 08:58 AM. Defendant not present.
	7	WAISD	**Bench warrant ordered issued for defendant. Bail set at $40, 000.00, Bailable. Night service: Yes**
	8	WAWSD	Bench warrant issued by David Gottlieb.
	9	BLBFN	Court orders bail bond # LG5-523993 FORFEITED.
	10	OFMCD	Minutes of T. Gonzales entered by Delia A on 06/18/2007.

Superior Court of California, County of Fresno

DOCKET REPORT

Case : F07904397 F A

Name : ██████████████████████

Date of Action	Seq Nbr	Code	Text
06/19/07			
	1	CLCST2	Defendant at counter to set Failure to Appear re: Arraignment set on 07/09/2007 at 08:30 AM in Department CRIM-B102.
	2	FIRAB	Letter of reassumption of surety bond filed.
07/09/07			
	1	CLCAN	FTA ARGN set on 07/09/07 at 08:30 AM in B102 has been cancelled.
	2	CLADD	Case calendared on 07/09/07 at 08:30 AM in Department 32, 3rd Floor for FTA Arraignment.
	3	HHELD	Hearing held on 7/9/2007 at 08:30:00 AM in Department 32, 3rd Floor for Failure to Appear Arraignment.
	4	OFJUD	Judicial Officer: Gottlieb, David, Judge
	5	OFJA	Courtroom Clerk: Gonzales, Tricia
	6	OFREP	Court Reporter: Lucy Blevins
	7	APDPD	Court appoints Public Defender to represent Defendant.
	8	APPDD	Public Defender Marina P Pincus appearing with defendant.
	9	APDDA	People present and are represented by, P Cheong, Deputy District Attorney.
	10	DFCRC	Copy of Complaint given to Defendant.
	11	ADWRA	The defendant waives reading of the complaining document, waives formal arraignment and waives reading of constitutional and statutory rights.
	12	PLNGA	Defendant waives reading of the Original Complaint, constitutional and statutory rights NG not guilty to all counts.
	13	WVTIM	Defendant waives statutory time for Preliminary Hearing.
	14	WVTGN	Defendant enters general time waiver. 10/60
	15	CLSET2	Pre Prelim re: Pre Prelim set on 07/24/2007 at 08:30 AM in Department 32, 3rd Floor.
	16	DSOTBP	Defendant is ordered to be present at next hearing.
	17	WAREC	Warrant issued on 06/18/2007 ordered recalled for defendant.
	18	JLTXT	Surety Bond reinstatement letter filed.
	19	SVBBFF	Court orders bail bond forfeiture for bond # LG5-523993 vacated. Bond ordered reinstated.
	20	DSCSR	Defendant remains surety bond.

DOCKET REPORT

Case : F07904397 F A

Name : ████████████████████████

Date of Action	Seq Nbr	Code	Text
07/09/07			
	21	OFMCD	Minutes of T. GONZALES entered by A LY on 07/09/2007.
07/24/07			
	1	HHELD	**Hearing held on 7/24/2007 at 08:30:00 AM in Department 32, 3rd Floor for Pre Prelim Pre Prelim.**
	2	OFJUD	Judicial Officer: Gottlieb, David, Judge
	3	OFJA	Courtroom Clerk: Gonzales, Tricia
	4	OFREP	Court Reporter: Oftedal, Lupe
	5	APPDD	Public Defender Todd D Eilers appearing with defendant.
	6	APDDA	People present and are represented by, Ed Browne, Deputy District Attorney.
	7	CT17B	Pursuant to Section 17 of the Penal Code, with approval of the Court and consent of the defendant, and by stipulation of counsel, this Court determines that the offense alleged in the complaint, Count 2, 484e(d) PC, is a misdemeanor, and further, that this case shall proceed as if the defendant has been arraigned on a misdemeanor complaint.
	8	PLWDA	Defendant motions to withdraw plea.
	9	PLWTH	**Defendant's motion to WITHDRAW NOT GUILTY PLEA to count(s) 2 granted.**
	10	PLNCT	**Defendant waives reading of the Original Complaint constitutional and statutory rights. NOLO CONTENDERE as to count(s) 2. Court finds there is factual basis for the plea and accepts the Nolo Contendere plea.**
	11	FICOP	The change of plea form is signed and filed in open court. Court accepts the plea and finds it was made knowingly, intelligently and voluntarily and that the plea is supported by a factual basis (People v West).
	12	DFADV	Defendant advised of rights in open court.
	13	CDCDM	Count(s) 1, 3, 4 DISMISSED - Other reason.
	14	WVFALC	Defendant waives time and formal arraignment for judgment and sentencing and states there is no legal cause why judgment should not be pronounced.
	15	WVTFS	The defendant waives statutory time for sentencing.
	16	PBGRT	The Court grants probation.
	17	PRISS	Imposition of judgment and sentence is suspended for a period of 3 Years and defendant is placed on 3 Years CONDITIONAL SENTENCE probation for count(s) 2 on the following terms and conditions as ordered by the Court:

DOCKET REPORT

Case : F07904397 F A

Name :

Date of Action	Seq Nbr	Code	Text
07/24/07			
	18	SEJAL	As to count(s) 2, defendant to serve 40 Days Fresno County Jail.
	19	JLSTA	Court grants jail stay until 11/02/2007 at 07:00 PM, Fresno County Jail.
	20	DFRTP	Defendant referred to Adult Offender Work Program.
	21	COACT	Report to the ACTION Center as directed by the court.
	22	JLCTS1	Credit for time served 3, actual 3, goodtime/worktime 0, treatment 0.
	23	SEFIN2	As to count(s) 2, pay a FINE of $470.00.
	24	SESEC	Pursuant to Penal Code 1465.8, a Court Security Fee is owed to the Court and included in the current balance.
	25	SEFEE	Pay FEE of $100.00 Restitution Fund PC 1202.4.
	26	ADATC	Pursuant to Penal Code 1202.44, defendant advised that if Probation is revoked an additional $100.00 will be ordered.
	27	STPYS	Payments to be paid at the rate of $35.00 per month beginning 09/04/2007 and on the 4 of each month thereafter until paid in full. $35.00 installment fee will be added to balance of fine.
	28	PROBY	Obey all laws.
	29	PRDIR	Defendant to obey all orders of the Probation Officer and report as directed.
	30	PRSAS	Submit to search and seizure of your person, residence, vehicle or any property under your control at any time of the day or night by any law enforcement or probation officer with or without a warrant, and with or without reasonable cause or reasonable suspicion.
	31	PRCHA	Report change of address to the Court and/or Probation within 7 days.
	32	PRDRG	Do not use drugs.
	33	PRNCC	Do not possess any checking account or fictitious writing instruments without the permission of the Probation Officer or the Court.
	34	TEXT	Or any ficticious writing instruments
	35	PRPRP	Defendant not to possess unlawful property.
	36	DSRFC	Defendant released on probation.
	37	BLBXN	Court orders surety bond # LG5-523993 exonerated.
	38	OFMCD	Minutes of T. Gonzales entered by Delia A on 07/24/2007.

DOCKET REPORT

Case : F07904397 F A

Name : ████████████████

Date of Action	Seq Nbr	Code	Text
07/25/07			
	1	BLBBNS	Bail Bond Notice Bail Bond Exoneration Sent for Bond # LG5-523993
08/10/07			
	1	COJUS	Clerk's office mailed JUS8715 form.
09/18/07			
	1	WCFTPW	Defendant has failed to pay, case to be reviewed for failure to pay action.
09/19/07			
	1	WCPDN	Defendant failed to pay, warning letter sent.
10/02/07			
	1	REMRC	Remittance from receipt # 1186331 received in the amount of $ 35.00.
11/05/07			
	1	WCFTP	Initiate FTP action identification.
11/06/07			
	1	WCPWQ	Schedule case for potential warrant work queue - FTP Not Hold Eligible
11/22/07			
	1	NTSNT	Courtesy Notice - FTP letter sent.
02/19/08			
	1	CLSET2	**Probation Hearing re: Modification set on 03/10/2008 at 01:30 PM in Department 11, B1 Floor.**
03/10/08			
	1	MOTION	Motion taken off calendar set in error to Dept. 11.
	2	HHELD	**Hearing held on 03/10/2008 at 01:30 AM in Department 11, B1 Floor for Probation Hearing Modification.**
	3	OFJUD	Judicial Officer: W Kent Hamlin, Judge
	4	OFJA	Courtroom Clerk: G. Broome
	5	OFREP	Court Reporter: Noelle Acosta
	6	CLOFF	Case taken off calendar.
	7	TEXT	Case set in wrong department. No appearance by defendant. Case taken off calendar, no action taken.
04/04/08			
	1	FIRPT	Report filed from AOWP.

DOCKET REPORT

Case : F07904397 F A

Name :

Date of Action	Seq Nbr	Code	Text
04/04/08			
	2	COFFJ	Clerk's Office forwards case to Judicial Officer Alvin Harrell for consideration. FTA/AOWP.
04/08/08			
	1	JLWARR	Jail Warrant issued. Defendant to serve 25 days in Fresno County Jail.
12/09/08			
	1	CLSET2	**Probation Hearing re: VOP Arraignment set on 12/10/2008 at 08:30 AM in Department 33, 3rd Floor.**
	2	TEXT	Per request of DA
12/10/08			
	1	HHELD	**Hearing held on 12/10/2008 at 08:30:00 AM in Department 33, 3rd Floor for Probation Hearing VOP Arraignment.**
	2	OFJUD	Judicial Officer: Whitehead, Denise, Judge
	3	OFJA	Courtroom Clerk: Lawson, Ginger
	4	OFREP	Court Reporter: Oftedal, Lupe
	5	APPDD	Public Defender Mari Anita Torres appearing with defendant.
	6	APDDA	People present and are represented by, Greg Strickland, Deputy District Attorney.
	7	JLTXT	**Per Jail records defendant is serving time on jail warrant (no bail) until 12/25/08**
	8	CLSET2	**Hearing re: For Reference Only set on 12/29/2008 at 08:30 AM in Department 33, 3rd Floor.**
	9	DSOTBP	Defendant is ordered to be present at next hearing.
	10	DSCSR	**Defendant remains in custody.**
	11	OFMCD	Minutes of G.Lawson entered by L.Embrey on 12/10/2008.
	12	NTJAL	Notice to Sheriff issued.
12/29/08			
	1	HHELD	**Hearing held on 12/29/2008 at 08:30:00 AM in Department 33, 3rd Floor for Hearing For Reference Only.**
	2	OFJUD	Judicial Officer: Whitehead, Denise, Judge
	3	OFJA	Courtroom Clerk: Lawson, Ginger
	4	OFREP	Court Reporter: Loring, Catherine
	5	APPDD	Public Defender Mari Anita Torres appearing with defendant.

DOCKET REPORT

Case : F07904397 F A

Name : █████████████████████

Date of Action	Seq Nbr	Code	Text
12/29/08			
	6	APDDA	People present and are represented by, Scott Sanders, Deputy District Attorney.
	7	APBOT	Probation Officer, present in court. K. Davis.
	8	COCTR	Court orders this case to trail case F08907500.
	9	PBTCR	Court orders probation reinstated, same terms and conditions.
	10	PBMOD	Conditional Probation modified as follows:
	11	PRRJR	The Court reserves jurisdiction over the issue of restitution to be paid to victim(s).
	12	PBTRM	Court orders probation terminated as to count(s) 2.
	13	DSRFC	Defendant released on all counts.
	14	OFMCD	Minutes of G.Lawson entered by L.Embrey on 12/29/2008.
	15	COSUB	Clerk's office sends JUS8715 subsequent action form to the Department of Justice.
01/14/13			
	1	WAFTP	Defendant failed to pay fine on 10/04/2007. Failure to Pay hold issued.
01/15/13			
	1	GCSER	Case Sent to Collections

copy of the original on file in this office

ATTEST: SEP 0 2 2014

State of California County of Fresno
Superior Court Clerk.
By_____, Deputy

Brian D. Lerner (Bar No. 158536)
Christopher A. Reed (Bar No. 235438)
Law Offices of Brian D. Lerner, APC
3233 E. Broadway
Long Beach, California 90803
Telephone: (562) 495-0554
Facsimile: (562) 608-8672

Attorneys for Respondent

UNITED STATES DEPARTMENT OF JUSTICE

EXECUTIVE OFFICE FOR IMMIGRATION REVIEW

IMMIGRATION COURT

LOS ANGELES, CALIFORNIA

In the Matter of:	
██████████████████	File No: ████████████
Respondent,	
In Removal Proceedings.	

Immigration Judge: Monica Little   Next Hearing: October 27, 2016 at 1:00 p.m.

**SUPPLEMENTAL DOCUMENTS FOR APPLICATION FOR CANCELLATION OF
REMOVAL FOR CERTAIN PERMANENT RESIDENTS**

TABLE OF CONTENTS

EXHIBIT '11'

Respondent's Daughter's Birth Certificate

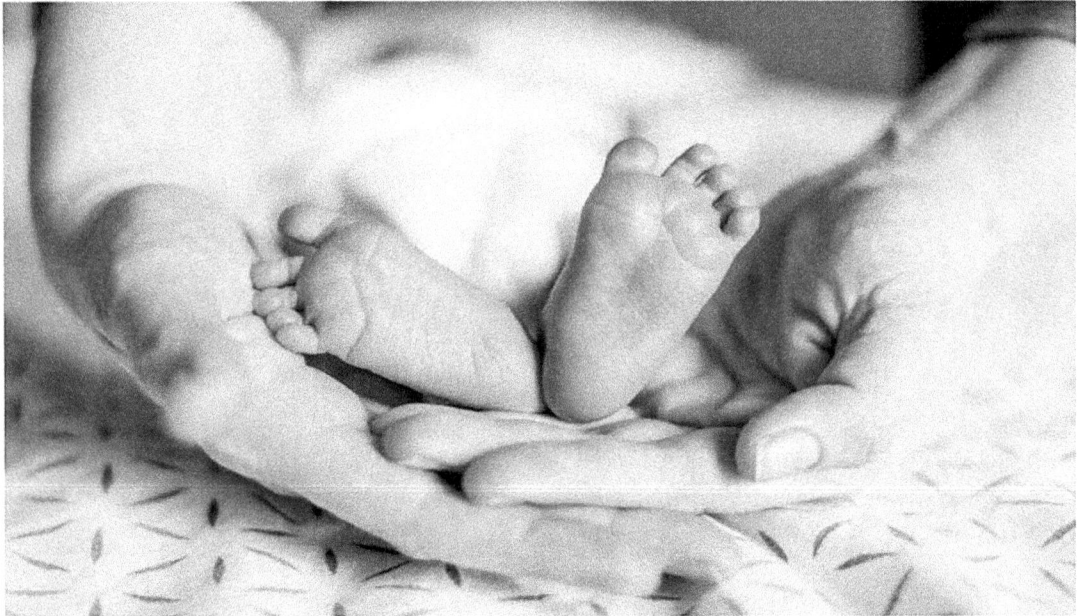

COUNTY of FRESNO
DEPARTMENT OF PUBLIC HEALTH
FRESNO, CALIFORNIA

CERTIFICATE OF LIVE BIRTH
STATE OF CALIFORNIA
USE BLACK INK ONLY

1201510008760

STATE FILE NUMBER			LOCAL REGISTRATION NUMBER
1A. NAME OF CHILD - FIRST ▉	1B. MIDDLE ▉	1C. LAST ▉	
2. SEX FEMALE	3A. THIS BIRTH, SINGLE, TWIN, ETC. SINGLE	3B. IF MULTIPLE, THIS CHILD 1ST, 2ND, ETC. -	4A. DATE OF BIRTH - MM/DD/CCYY 07/11/2015	4B. HOUR - 24 HOUR CLOCK TIME 1320
5A. PLACE OF BIRTH - NAME OF HOSPITAL OR FACILITY CLOVIS COMMUNITY HOSPITAL		5B. STREET ADDRESS - STREET AND NUMBER OR LOCATION ▉		
5C. CITY CLOVIS		5D. COUNTY FRESNO		
6A. NAME OF FATHER/PARENT - FIRST -	6B. MIDDLE -	6C. LAST -	7. BIRTHPLACE - STATE/COUNTRY	8. DATE OF BIRTH - MM/DD/CCYY
9A. NAME OF MOTHER/PARENT - FIRST ▉	9B. MIDDLE ▉	9C. LAST - BIRTH NAME ▉	10. BIRTHPLACE - STATE/COUNTRY PHILIPPINES	11. DATE OF BIRTH - MM/DD/CCYY 01/26/1979
11. I CERTIFY THAT I HAVE REVIEWED THE STATED INFORMATION AND THAT IT IS TRUE AND CORRECT TO THE BEST OF MY KNOWLEDGE. *(signature)*	12A. PARENT OR OTHER INFORMANT - SIGNATURE		12B. RELATIONSHIP TO CHILD MOTHER	12C. DATE SIGNED - MM/DD/CCYY 07/14/2015
I CERTIFY THAT THE CHILD WAS BORN ALIVE AT THE DATE, HOUR, AND PLACE STATED.	13A. ATTENDANT/CERTIFIER - SIGNATURE AND DEGREE OR TITLE *A. Clark, Birth Clerk*		13B. LICENSE NUMBER A350410	13C. DATE SIGNED - MM/DD/CCYY 07/14/2015
13D. TYPED NAME, TITLE AND MAILING ADDRESS OF ATTENDANT GOPAL R GADE, MD, 6183 N FRESNO #105, FRESNO			14. TYPED NAME AND TITLE OF CERTIFIER IF OTHER THAN ATTENDANT A. CLARK, BIRTH CLERK	
15A. DATE OF DEATH - MM/DD/CCYY	15B. STATE FILE NO - STATE USE ONLY	16. LOCAL REGISTRAR - SIGNATURE KENNETH BIRD, M.D.	17. DATE ACCEPTED FOR REGISTRATION - MM/DD/CCYY 07/22/2015	

EXHIBIT '12'

Proof of Biometrics

Department of Homeland Security
U.S. Citizenship and Immigration Ser[...]

rm I-797C, Notice of Action

THIS NOTICE DOES NOT GRANT ANY IMMIGRATION STATUS OR BENEFIT.

ASC Appointment Notice	APPLICATION/PETITION/REQUEST NUMBER SRC1423750478		NOTICE DATE 09/05/2014
CASE TYPE I485 - APPLICATION TO REGISTER PERMANENT RESIDENCE OR ADJUST STATUS	SOCIAL SECURITY NUMBER	USCIS A# A042049242	CODE 3
ACCOUNT NUMBER	TCR	SERVICE CENTER TSC	PAGE 1 of 1

C/O [REDACTED]
200 S LOMA DR 3
LOS ANGELES CA 90026

To process your application, petition, or request, the U. S. Citizenship & Immigration Services (USCIS) must capture your biometrics.
PLEASE APPEAR AT THE BELOW APPLICATION SUPPORT CENTER AT THE DATE AND TIME SPECIFIED.
IF YOU FAIL TO APPEAR AS SCHEDULED, YOUR APPLICATION, PETITION, OR REQUEST WILL BE CONSIDERED ABANDONED.

APPLICATION SUPPORT CENTER	PLEASE READ THIS ENTIRE NOTICE CAREFULLY.
USCIS WILSHIRE	DATE AND TIME OF APPOINTMENT
1015 WILSHIRE BOULEVARD 1ST FLOOR, SUITE 100	09/23/2014
LOS ANGELES CA 90017	03:00PM

WHEN YOU GO TO THE APPLICATION SUPPORT CENTER TO HAVE YOUR BIOMETRICS TAKEN, YOU MUST BRING:
1. **THIS APPOINTMENT NOTICE** and
2. **PHOTO IDENTIFICATION.** Naturalization applicants must bring their Alien Resident Card. All other applicants must bring a passport, driver's license, national ID, military ID, or State-issued photo ID. If you appear without proper identification, you will not be fingerprinted.

CELL PHONES, CAMERAS, OR OTHER RECORDING DEVICES ARE NOT PERMITTED.

REQUEST FOR RESCHEDULING

☐ **Please reschedule my appointment.** Once USCIS receives your request, you will be sent a new appointment notice. Make a copy of this notice for your records, then mail the original with your request to BPU, Alexandria ASC, Suite 100, 8850 Richmond Hwy, Alexandria, VA 22309-1586

BIOMETRICS PROCESSING STAMP
ASC SITE CODE
BIOMETRICS CAPTURED ON
91967
BIOMETRICS CA REVIEW BY
91967
SEP 23 2014

APPLICATION NUMBER
I485 - SRC1423750478

If you have any questions regarding this notice, please call 1-800-375-5283.
WARNING: *Due to limited seating availability in our lobby area, only persons who are necessary to assist with transportation or completing the biometrics worksheet should accompany you. If you have open wounds or bandages/casts when you appear, the USCIS may reschedule your appointment if it is determined your injuries will interfere with taking your biometrics.*

EXHIBIT '13'

Respondent's Updated California Criminal History Information
(CALDOJ)

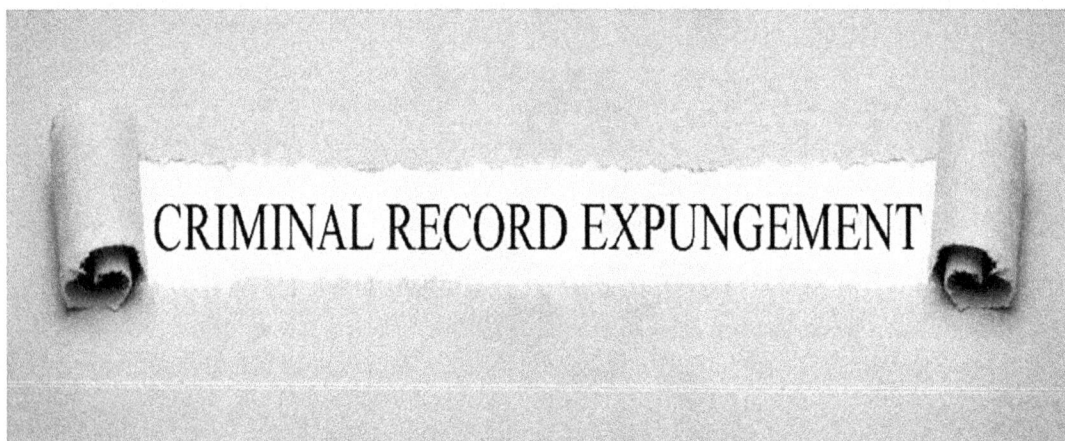

KAMALA D. HARRIS
Attorney General

State of California
DEPARTMENT OF JUSTICE

BUREAU OF CRIMINAL INFORMATION AND ANALYSIS
P.O. Box 903417
SACRAMENTO, CA 94203-4170

May 10, 2016

██████████████

RE: California Criminal History Information

Dear Applicant:

This is in response to your record review request concerning the existence of a California criminal history record maintained in the files of the Department of Justice's Bureau of Criminal Information and Analysis. Your fingerprints did identify to an existing California criminal history record and a copy of that record is enclosed. If you wish to challenge the accuracy or completeness of your record, please complete and return the enclosed form (BCIA 8706) and supporting documentation to the address noted above.

Pursuant to California Penal Code section 11121, the purpose of a record review request is to afford an individual with a copy of their record and to refute any erroneous or inaccurate information contained therein. The intent is not to be used for licensing, certification or employment purposes.

Additionally, California Penal Code sections 11125, 11142, and 11143 does not allow for a person or agency to make a request to another person to provide them with a copy of an individual's criminal history or notification that a record does not exist; does not allow an authorized person to furnish the record to an unauthorized person; nor does it allow an unauthorized person to buy, receive or possess the record or information. A violation of these section codes is a misdemeanor.

Sincerely,

Cindy Santos

Record Review Unit
Applicant Information and Certification Program
Bureau of Criminal Information and Analysis

For KAMALA D. HARRIS
Attorney General

Enclosures
BCIA 8711 (Rev. 06/10)

64 | P a g e

4CMTDP298338.IH
RE: QHY.CA0349400.28402571 PUSR. DATE:20160510 TIME:(37:28
RESTRICTED-DO NOT USE FOR EMPLOYMENT,LICENSING OR CERTIFICATION PURPOSES
ATTN:APPUSR

****
FOR CALIFORNIA AGENCIES ONLY - HAS PREVIOUS QUALIFYING OFFENSE. COLLECT
DNA IF INCARCERATED, CONFINED, OR ON PROBATION OR PAROLE FOLLOWING ANY
MISDEMEANOR OR FELONY CONVICTION. REQUEST KITS AND INFO AT (510) 620-
3300 OR PC296.PC296@DOJ.CA.GOV.
****
** PALM PRINT ON FILE AT DOJ FOR ADDITIONAL INFORMATION PLEASE E-MAIL
PALM.PRINT@DOJ.CA.GOV
** III CALIFORNIA ONLY SOURCE RECORD
CII/A28402571
DOB/19790126   SEX/F RAC/HISPANIC
HGT/500 WGT/160 EYE/BRO HAI/BRO POB/PI
CTZ/PHILIPPINES
NAM/001
   002 ██████████████

FBI/679551RC6
DMV/B7612926
SOC/607221783
SMT/TAT BACK-UNKNOWN   ; TAT L ANKL-UNKNOWN   ;
    TAT R SHLD-UNKNOWN
* * * *

ARR/DET/CITE: NAM:001 DOB:19790126
20070602   CAPD FRESNO

CNT:001   #0766634-428787
  470(D) PC-FALSE CHECKS/RECORDS/CERTS/ETC   TOC:F
   SCN:S49A1530023
- - - -
COURT: NAM:001
20070724 CASC FRESNO CENTRAL

CNT:001   #F107904397
  470(D) PC-FALSE CHECKS/RECORDS/CERTS/ETC   TOC:F
 DISPO:DISMISSED

CNT:002
  530.5(A) PC-GET CREDIT/ETC:USE OTHER'S ID   TOC:F
 DISPO:DISMISSED

CNT:003
  496(A) PC-RECEIVE/ETC KNOWN STOLEN PROPERTY   TOC:F
 DISPO:DISMISSED

CNT:004
  484E(D) PC-USE ACCESS ACCOUNT INFO W/O CONSENT   TOC:F
*DISPO:CONVICTED
  CONV STATUS:MISDEMEANOR
   SEN: 036 MONTHS PROBATION, 003 DAYS JAIL, 003 DAYS JAIL OR FINE,
       FINE, RESTN

 DISPO:CONVICTION CERT BY CLERK OF THE COURT
 DISPO:FOR CERT INFO SEE AUTOMATED ARCHIVE SYS

20081229
 DISPO:EARLY DISMISSAL FROM PROBATION
* * * *

```
ARR/DET/CITE:           NAM:001  DOB:19790126
20080325    CAPD FRESNO

CNT:001      #0886809-428787
  11377(A) HS-POSSESS CONTROLLED SUBSTANCE           TOC:F

CNT:002
  11550(A) HS-USE/UNDER INFL CONTRLD SUBSTANCE       TOC:M
   SCN:S49B0850009
- - - -
COURT:                  NAM:001
20080514   CASC FRESNO CENTRAL

CNT:001      #F08902017
  11550(A) HS-USE/UNDER INFL CONTRLD SUBSTANCE       TOC:M
 DISPO:DISMISSED

CNT:002
  11377(A) HS-POSSESS CONTROLLED SUBSTANCE           TOC:F
 DISPO:PROC SUSP/DRUG CRT-DEFERRED JUDGEMENT

20081229
 DISPO:DRG CRT/DEFER JDGMNT-TRM CRM PROC REINST
- - - -
COURT:                  NAM:001
20081229   CASC FRESNO CENTRAL

CNT:001      #F08902017
  11377(A) HS-POSSESS CONTROLLED SUBSTANCE           TOC:F
*DISPO:CONVICTED
   CONV STATUS:FELONY
    SEN: 024 MONTHS PROBATION, 002 DAYS JAIL, WORK PROGRAM, IMP SEN SS

 DISPO:COND OF PROB-DRUG TREATMENT PLACEMENT
* * * *

ARR/DET/CITE:           NAM:001  DOB:19790126
20081201    CAPD FRESNO

CNT:001      #08103848-428787
  11377(A) HS-POSSESS CONTROLLED SUBSTANCE           TOC:F

CNT:002
  11364 HS-POSSESS CONTROL SUBSTANCE PARAPHERNA      TOC:M

CNT:003
  12316(B)(1) PC-PROHIBITED OWN/ETC AMMO/ETC         TOC:F
   ADR:20081201 (200,LOMA, ,S,LA,CA,90026)
    SCN:S49B3360019
- - - -
COURT:                  NAM:001
20081229   CASC FRESNO CENTRAL

CNT:001      #F08907500
  11364 HS-POSSESS CONTROL SUBSTANCE PARAPHERNA      TOC:M
 DISPO:DISMISSED

CNT:002
  11377(A) HS-POSSESS CONTROLLED SUBSTANCE           TOC:F
*DISPO:CONVICTED
   CONV STATUS:FELONY
    SEN: 024 MONTHS PROBATION, 001 DAYS JAIL, WORK PROGRAM, IMP SEN SS

 DISPO:COND OF PROB-DRUG TREATMENT PLACEMENT
```

EXHIBIT '14'

Fresno County Sheriff's Department Arrest Report, California Superior
Court Criminal Complaint and Plea Form (F07904397)

R 07904397

FRESNO COUNTY SHERIFF'S DEPARTMENT ARREST REPORT

Booking No:	JID:	Name(Last, First Middle):	Area:	Zone:	Report Number:
		██████████	NW	2048	07047548 - 1

Street Address:		City:	Zip Code:	Yrs / Mos:	Residence Phone:	Alias:
310 G ST		FRESNO	93721			

Race:	Age:	Sex:	Eye Color:	Hair Color:	Wgt:	Hgt:	DOB:	Eth:	POB - City:	POB - State:
A	28	F	BRO	BLK	100	500	01/26/1979		PHILLAPINES	

Scars/marks/tattoos:
TAT R SHD BUTTERFLY KISSING FLOWER / TAT L ANK FLOWER W/DESIGN / TAT BACK TINKER BELL

SSN:	Drvr.Lic.#:	St:	FBI No:	SID No:	CDC No:	
	B7612926	CA				

Arrival Date:	Arrival Time:	Arrest Date:	Arrest Time:	Arrest Location:
		06/02/2007	21:55	3259 N DEWEY AV / W FEDORA AV

Arrest Agency:	Arrest Officer:	Comp. #:
FPD	WALKER (V3273), KIM - P1222	

Transporting Officer:	Agency:	From:	To:
WALKER (V3273), KIM - P1222	PD	LOA	I BUREAU

Transporting Officer:	Agency:	From:	To:
-	PD	I BUREAU	FCJ

Blood Alcohol Level:	Condition:	Attitude:	Employer Name:	Occupation:
	OK	COOPERATIVE		NONE

Hair Length:	Hair Style:	Facial Hair:	Complexion:	Build:	Clothing:
SHLDR	STRAIGHT		MEDIUM	THIN	JEANS,BROWN TANK TOP

Nearest Relative or Friend:	Address:	Phone:
NONE		

Injury/Illness:	Medical Attention:	
NONE STATED		

License:	State:	Year:	Make:	Model:	Color:	Released To:

Arrest Details:
SUBJECT WAS CONTACTED AT RESIDENCE AND FOUND TO HAVE SEVERAL ALTERED CHECKS IN HER POSSESSION.

The above offense(s) was/were committed in my presence and under the authority of California Penal Code section 837, I hereby arrest and deliver to the Fresno County Sheriff's Department for Transportation and Booking, the above listed suspect on the above listed charges. I have knowledge that knowingly making a false arrest is a criminal offense (Cal. P.C. 148.5).

Signature of Arresting Citizen   Address   Phone

Signature of Person Being Arrested   Left Thumb: Right Thumb:

FRESNO COUNTY SHERIFF'S DEPARTMENT ARREST REPORT

Booking No:	JID:	Name (Last, First Middle):		Area:	Zone:	Report Number:
		███████████		NW	2048	07047548 - 1

Street Address:		City:	Zip Code:	Yrs / Mos:	Residence Phone:	Alias:
310 G ST		FRESNO	93721			

Race:	Age:	Sex:	Eye Color:	Hair Color:	Wgt:	Hgt:	DOB:	Eth:	POB - City:	POB - State:
A	28	F	BRO	BLK	100	500	01/26/1979		PHILLAPINES	

Charge:	Counts:	Drug Weight/Amount:
PC 470(D)	1	

Warrant No:	Judicial District:	Judge:	DOI:	Bail Amount:
	FRESNO MUNI			

SUPERIOR COURT OF CALIFORNIA, COUNTY OF FRESNO
CENTRAL DIVISION

FILED

JUN 0 5 2007

FRESNO COUNTY SUPERIOR COURT

By_____ DEPUTY

THE PEOPLE OF THE STATE OF
CALIFORNIA,

                                    Plaintiff

                    vs.

████████████████████

                                    Defendant(s)

COMPLAINT - CRIMINAL

FELONY COMPLAINT

COURT CASE NO.   07904397

DA FILE NO. 2007F22182

OIF 10 47,00

Agency: Fresno Police Department

Agency Report Number: 07-47548

Defendant	Birth Date	Booking No.
████████████████	01/26/1979	07-10171

Personally appeared before me, who first being duly sworn, complains and alleges:

COUNT 1

On or about June 2, 2007, in the above named judicial district, the crime of FORGERY, in violation of PENAL CODE SECTION 470(d), a felony, was committed by Anna Carissa Estaya Unlayao, who did, with the intent to defraud, falsely make, alter, forge and counterfeit, utter, publish, pass and attempt to offer to pass, as true and genuine, Checks, knowing the same to be false, altered, forged and counterfeited.

*****

COUNT 2

On or about June 2, 2007, in the above named judicial district, the crime of ACQUISITION OF ACCESS CARD ACCOUNT INFORMATION, in violation of PENAL CODE SECTION 484e(d), a felony, was committed by ████████████████ who acquired and retained possession of access card account information with respect to an access card validly issued to another person, without the cardholder's and issuer's consent, with intent to use it fraudulently.

*****

COUNT 3

On or about June 2, 2007, in the above named judicial district, the crime of IDENTITY THEFT, in violation of PENAL CODE SECTION 530.5(a), a felony, was committed by Anna Carissa Estaya Unlayao, who did willfully obtain personal identifying information on ████████████████ and unlawfully use that information to obtain, and attempt to obtain, credit, goods and services in the name of, ████████████ without consent.

*****

COUNT 4

On or about June 2, 2007, in the above named judicial district, the crime of RECEIVING STOLEN PROPERTY - PERSONAL PROPERTY, in violation of PENAL CODE SECTION 496(a), a felony, was committed by Anna Carissa Estaya Unlayao, who did unlawfully buy, receive, conceal, sell, withhold, or aid in concealing, selling, or withholding personal property belonging to ████████ ████████which had been stolen, knowing that said property had been stolen.

*****

All of which is contrary to the form, force, and effect of the Statute in such case made and provided, and against the peace and dignity of the people of the State of California.

* * * * *

Pursuant to Penal Code Sections 1054.5(b), the People are hereby informally requesting that defense counsel provide discovery to the People as required by Penal Code Section 1054.3.

Pursuant to Penal Code Section 1054.2, no attorney may disclose or permit to be disclosed to a defendant, members of the defendant's family, or anyone else, the address or telephone number of a victim or witness whose name is disclosed pursuant to Penal Code Section 1054.1(a), unless ordered by the court. Willful violation of this section by an attorney, persons employed by an attorney, or persons appointed by the court is a misdemeanor.

The People of the State of California hereby give notice that the prosecution will allege and prove any and all applicable California Rules of Court, Rule 4.421 facts in aggravation pursuant to *Blakely v. Washington,* 542 U.S. 296 (2004) and *Cunningham v. California,* 542 U.S. ___ [2007 WL 135687]. The People of the State of California will allege said aggravating factors in the Information and hereby further reserve the right to present any and all applicable aggravating facts conforming to proof at trial.

Subscribed and sworn to before me on

DATE: _____

Attest:

_____
DEPUTY CLERK

_____
COMPLAINANT

SUPERIOR COURT OF CALIFORNIA • COUNTY OF FRESNO
1100 Van Ness Avenue
Fresno, California 93724-0002

FILED

40 days

FRESNO COUNTY SUPERIOR COURT

DEPUTY

PLAINTIFF: PEOPLE OF THE STATE OF CALIFORNIA

DEFENDANT: ████████████

MISDEMEANOR ADVISEMENT, WAIVER OF RIGHTS, AND PLEA FORM	CASE NUMBER: F 0790 4 39 7

I understand the nature of the charges against me and I request to withdraw my plea(s) of not guilty and now plead ☐ GUILTY ☒ NO CONTEST to the following violation(s) of law (list counts, code sections, priors, and any conditions of the plea):

PC 984 e (1)

RIGHT TO AN ATTORNEY:
I understand I have the right to be represented by an attorney at all stages of the proceedings, and if I am unable to afford an attorney, the court will appoint one for me.

1. I have had enough time to discuss my case and all possible defenses with my attorney . . . .

2. I GIVE UP MY RIGHT to have an attorney represent me. . . . .

CONSTITUTIONAL RIGHTS:
I understand I am presumed innocent and the State is required to prove me guilty beyond a reasonable doubt. I also understand that I have the following constitutional rights as to all matters charged against me:

	I understand this right	I give up this right
1. The right to a speedy, public JURY or COURT TRIAL.		
2. The right to be CONFRONTED by WITNESSES against me; that is, to see, hear and question all witnesses against me.		
3. The right to NOT INCRIMINATE MYSELF; that is, not to be compelled to testify against myself though I may testify if I choose to do so.		
4. The right to PRESENT EVIDENCE at no cost to me and to have the court issue subpenas to bring into court all witnesses and evidence favorable to me.		

CONSEQUENCES OF PLEA OF GUILTY OR NO CONTEST: I understand:

1. If I am presently on parole or probation, my change of plea could be a reason for finding me in violation of my parole or probation. . . . .

2. If I am not a citizen, my change of plea can result in my deportation, exclusion from admission to the United States, and/or a denial of naturalization. Deportation may be mandatory for this offense. I have fully discussed this my attorney and understand the serious immigration consequences of my plea. . . . .

3. The maximum sentence I can receive as a result of my plea   1 yr + $2,000

4. Other possible consequences of this plea will include a restitution fine of $100 to $1000, and may include (e.g. registration): _____

5. The facts on which I base my plea are: _people v. ▮▮▮▮_   [initials]

6. I am entering my plea freely and voluntarily without fear or threat to me or anyone closely related to me. . . . . [initials]

7. The matter of probation and sentence is to be determined solely by the Court. . . . . [initials]

8. I understand that I have the right to wait a minimum of six hours, and up to five days to be sentenced. I give up this right and agree to be sentenced at this time. . . . . [initials]

9. I understand that I may be required to provide buccal swab samples and any blood specimens or other biological samples required for law enforcement identification analysis.   [☒]

I declare under PENALTY OF PERJURY, under the laws of the State of California, that I have read, understood, and initialed each item above, and everything on this form is true and correct.

Date: _7-24-07_   Signed: x _[signature]_
                                  (Defendant)

WAIVER OF PRESENCE/JUDGE

I hereby waive my right to be present and I authorize my attorney to enter the plea on my behalf. I agree to be sentenced at the time the plea is entered. I authorize my attorney to accept the court's orders and conditions on my behalf, if any, imposed on me.

I understand that I have the right to enter my plea before and be sentenced by a judge. I give up this right and agree to be sentenced by a temporary judge.

Date: _____   Signed: _____
                                  (Defendant)

ATTORNEY'S STATEMENT

I am the attorney of record for the defendant and have reviewed this form with my client. I have explained to the defendant of his/her rights and answered all of the defendant's questions with regard to this plea. I have discussed the facts the case with the defendant, and explained the consequences of this plea, the elements of the offense(s), and the possible defense(s). I concur with this plea and the defendant's decision to waive his/her constitutional rights.

Date: _7-24-07_   Signed: _[signature]_
                                  (Attorney for Defendant)

INTERPRETER'S STATEMENT (IF APPLICABLE)

I, _____, have been duly sworn and have truly translated this form to the defendant in the _____ language. The defendant indicated that (s)he understood the contents of the form, and (s)he has initialed the form.

Date: _____   Signed: _____
                                  (Court Interpreter)

COURT'S FINDINGS AND ORDER

The Court, having reviewed this form and having questioned the defendant concerning the defendant's constitutional rights, accepts the defendant's plea(s) and the factual basis for the plea(s), and finds that the defendant has expressly, knowingly, understandingly, and intelligently waived his/her constitutional rights. The Court finds that the defendant's plea(s) is freely and voluntarily made with an understanding of the nature and consequences of the plea(s). The defendant is convicted on the basis of his/her plea(s).

The Court orders this form filed and entered in this case.

Date: _7-24-07_   Signed: _[signature]_
                                  (Judge of Superior Court)

EXHIBIT '15'

Letter from Respondent's Mother

May 20, 2016

████████
██████████████

Dear Immigration Judge,

My name is ████████████████████████ I came to America in 1983. My siblings and I acquired our US citizenship as a derivatives of our father Santiago Estaya Sr. When we growing up in the Philippines we know that we are All American citizens. My father said because he was naturalized after the war in 1949 and granted the US citizenship in Batangas, Philippines. We often ask our father how did it happened, how he was granted the US citizenship, before he even came to America. He just answered with a smile. I always thought he was simply really a good man who love his family and his country. He was proud to be an American and so do us, his children. Some three years ago, out of curiosity I google my father's name, and to my amazement I found his name listed on the book titled "The Hour of Redemptions". This is about the Last raid in Cabanatuan, an effort to rescue more than 500 US soldiers POW'S. He was one of the Philippines Scout who helped the US Armed Forces. Now, I know why he was granted the US citizenship before he even step his feet on American soil. He was awarded the "Bronze Star for Heroic Achievement on January 30, 1945, along with it is also his US Naturalization. I am so very proud that I am his daughter.

My daughter ██████████████ is my father's youngest granddaughter when he passed away in December of 1982, if he is alive now it will break his heart to pieces to see his granddaughter to be deported. My daughter's family is here in United States. Her daughter ████ is here, it will be devastated to break them apart. Mila is her life. We don't want Mila to grow up without a mother. My husband and I and her siblings and her niece ████ are all here. Her bond with my other daughter ████ is exceptional they love each other so much. They always talked about the future of their kids growing up and raising them together.

Yes, she may have done some crazy things before, but she is change woman now. She worked hard as a caregiver and she is an excellent one. She went to school to become a drug counselor, but job is so scarce nowadays. And she love taking care of old folks, possibly reminding her of grandma and grandpa.

When I had my children in the Philippines, I thought my children are all citizen of the United States and will have the same status like myself. I was a very young mother, I had my 3 children before I marry their father. My mother last wished to me is not to marry right away because we were young and there is no divorce in the Philippines. So we decided not get married until October of 1984. When I went to US embassy in Manila they told me that I have to file a petition for them. During the years, I was working so, hard to make ends meet and I forgot to file a citizenship papers for them and because of my neglect Anna Carissa's s is subject to deportation. Please my heartfelt plea, Your Honor, please don't separate our family again. Anna Carissa and her daughter need to be here at the same place. Anna Carissa deserve another chance and let us be happy as one family and hopefully she will get her citizenship because I was unable to report and register them at the US Immigration in Manila after their birth, due to my innocence or lack of knowledge at that time. When eldest son Edmund and Anna Carissa they received their original Green Card it has no expiration date. I was robbed at a shopping Mall in the 1990's, and I have her original green card in my purse along with my other papers. So when I received a new one, I have my husband to hide it so it will not get lost again. Didn't realize until later on when she went to the cruise that there is an expiration date, who would have thought. And that is the reason why she is in this position right now.

Your Honor, please do not deport our daughter, this is the only home that she has ever known ever since she came here in 1990. It will be a great lost for her and her daughter to be separated from each and the family that loves her.

Respectfully,

EXHIBIT '16'

Letter of Employment

5/9/16

To Whom it May Concern,

This letter is to speak of the character of ▮▮▮▮▮▮▮▮▮▮▮ has worked for me at Around the Clock Companion Care since December 29th, 2015. I am the person responsible for hiring her and managing her as well as my other employees on a daily basis. Since she begun working for me, she has been very responsible, caring and dependable. Our elderly clients love her and our client's children feel very safe knowing that their parents are in good hands. With her current work ethic and motivated state of mind, I feel very confident that he will work for us for many years to come. I hope this letter helps speak of her tremendous character.

Thank you,

Brandon Miller
Staffing Supervisor
Around the Clock Care

(559) 320-2400
bmiller@bakersfieldcare.com

EXHIBIT '17'

Additional Letters of Support

California Association of Addiction Recovery Resources
P.O. Box 214127, Sacramento, CA 95821
916-338-9460 ~ FAX: 916-338-9468
TTY: 916-473-0836

KEEP THIS LETTER FOR YOUR RECORDS AND YOUR EMPLOYER!

January 19, 2012

████████████████

Dear ████

This letter confirms your CAS registration #11836. The State of California, Department of Alcohol and Drug Programs, Counselor Certification Regulations requires that you complete the certification process within FIVE years from the date of registration. Your date of registration is: 1/19/2012. You are current through: 12/31/2012.

Your registration will need to be renewed annually until you become certified. Every year you are required to have three hours total of ethics and confidentiality trainings.

Good luck with your certification process, and please contact us with any further questions or concerns.

Sincerely,

Ken Jones
Operations Director

www.caarr.org

ICDC COLLEGE®

MAIN CAMPUS
6812 PACIFIC BLVD
HUNTINGTON PARK CA 90255
TEL 323 277 0240 / FAX 323 277

CORPORATE HEADQUARTERS
11859 WILSHIRE BLVD STE 600
LOS ANGELES CA 90025
TEL 310 482 6996 / FAX 310 473 2048

CORPORATE / ONLINE OFFICE
5995 SEPULVEDA BLVD
CULVER CITY CA 90230
TEL 310 482 6996 / FAX 310 482

December 2, 2015

Immigration Judge
U. S. Department of Homeland Security
606 S Olive St Floor 16
Court Room 1
Los Angeles CA 90014-1660

Re: Character Reference for ██████████

The Honorable Immigration Judge,

I have known ████████████. since January 18, 2011. She graduated from the ICDC College 9-month Alcohol & Drug Counseling vocation program, and successfully completed her externship on November 2, 2011. Anna Unlayao was a good student, actively participated in group counseling sessions, learned the 12 core functions, and developed her documentation skills.

I can confirm that ██████ is a person of compassion and integrity. She is dedicated to her field of study and seeking gainful employment as a Substance Abuse Counselor.

Sincerely,

Victor Martinez
Career Advisor
ICDC College
6812 Pacific Blvd
Huntington Park CA 90255
(323) 277 0240 x325

DIPLOMA

PRESENTED TO

Has successfully completed a training course

Alcohol and Drug Counseling

at

ICDC COLLEGE

5422 Sunset Blvd.,
Hollywood, CA 90027

Revekka Gershler,
Executive Director

11/02/11
Date

Marina Frid,
Campus President, Hollywood Campus

11/02/11
Date

To Whom It May Concern:

My name is Cindy Streufert. I was born in Wantagh, N.Y and moved to Fresno Ca in 1980. I have lived in the United States all my life (56 years) and am a proud, legal citizen of the United States.

I've worked at Baker, Fraser, Sawyers LLP for 18 years. I've known Carissa for at least 15 of those years. She dated my oldest son for quite some time.

In all the years I have known Carissa she has been happy, polite, a hard worker & an extremely faithful young woman. I have also come to know her as a wonderful mother & friend — Sincerely,

Cindy Streufert

EXHIBIT '18'

Respondent's 2015 Income Tax Return

⚠ Make sure the SSN(s) above and on line 6c are correct.

Presidential Election Campaign
Check here if you, or your spouse if filing jointly, want $3 to go to this fund. Checking a box below will not change your tax or refund. ☐ You ☐ Spouse

Filing status
Check only one box.

1 ☒ Single
2 ☐ Married filing jointly (even if only one had income)
3 ☐ Married filing separately. Enter spouse's SSN above and full name here. ►
4 ☐ Head of household (with qualifying person). (See instructions.) If the qualifying person is a child but not your dependent, enter this child's name here. ►
5 ☐ Qualifying widow(er) with dependent child (see instructions)

Exemptions

6a ☒ Yourself. If someone can claim you as a dependent, do not check box 6a.

Boxes checked on 6a and 6b ► 1

b ☐ Spouse

c Dependents:

No. of children on 6c who:

(1) First name Last name	(2) Dependent's social security number	(3) Dependent's relationship to you	(4) ✓ if child under age 17 qualifying for child tax cr. (see inst.)
▮▮▮▮▮▮	▮▮▮▮▮▮	DAUGHTER	☒

If more than six dependents, see inst.

● lived with you ► 1

● did not live with you due to divorce or separation (see inst.)

Dependents on 6c not entered above

CLIENT COPY

d Total number of exemptions claimed.

Add numbers on lines above ► ☐ 2

Income

Attach Form(s) W-2 here. Also attach Form(s) 1099-R if tax was withheld.

If you did not get a W-2, see instructions.

7 Wages, salaries, tips, etc. Attach Form(s) W-2. ... 7 | 4,011

8a Taxable interest. Attach Schedule B if required. ... 8a
b Tax-exempt interest. Do not include on line 8a. 8b
9a Ordinary dividends. Attach Schedule B if required. ... 9a
b Qualified dividends (see instructions). 9b
10 Capital gain distributions (see instructions). ... 10
11a IRA distributions. 11a   11b Taxable amount (see instructions). 11b
12a Pensions and annuities. 12a   12b Taxable amount (see instructions). 12b
13 Unemployment compensation and Alaska Permanent Fund dividends. ... 13 | 1,365
14a Social security benefits. 14a   14b Taxable amount (see instructions). 14b
15 Add lines 7 through 14b (far right column). This is your **total income.** ► 15 | 5,376

Adjusted gross income

16 Educator expenses (see instructions). 16
17 IRA deduction (see instructions). 17
18 Student loan interest deduction (see instructions). 18
19 Tuition and fees. Attach Form 8917. 19
20 Add lines 16 through 19. These are your **total adjustments.** 20
21 Subtract line 20 from line 15. This is your **adjusted gross income.** ► 21 | 5,376

For Disclosure, Privacy Act, and Paperwork Reduction Act Notice, see separate instructions.   Form **1040A** (2015)

FDA   15 1040A1   BWF 1040   Form Software Copyright 1998 - 2016 HRB Tax Group, Inc.

85 | Page

	22	Enter the amount from line 21 (adjusted gross income).			22	5,376

Tax, credits, and payments

23a	Check if:	☐ You were born before Jan. 2, 1951, ☐ Blind	☐ Spouse was born before Jan. 2, 1951, ☐ Blind	Total boxes checked ▶ 23a		
b	If you are married filing separately and your spouse itemizes deductions, check here ▶ 23b ☐					

Standard Deduction for—

● People who check any box on line 23a or 23b or who can be claimed as a dependent, see instructions.

● All others:

Single or Married filing separately, $6,300

Married filing jointly or Qualifying widow(er), $12,600

Head of household, $9,250

24	Enter your standard deduction.				24	6,300
25	Subtract line 24 from line 22. If line 24 is more than line 22, enter -0-.				25	0
26	Exemptions. Multiply $4,000 by the number on line 6d.				26	8,000
27	Subtract line 26 from line 25. If line 26 is more than line 25, enter -0-. This is your taxable income.			▶ 27		0
28	Tax, including any alternative minimum tax (see inst.)		28	0		
29	Excess advance premium tax credit repayment. Attach Form 8962.		29			
30	Add lines 28 and 29.			30		
31	Credit for child and dependent care expenses. Attach Form 2441.		31			
32	Credit for the elderly or the disabled. Attach Schedule R.		32			
33	Education credits from Form 8863, line 19.		33			
34	Retirement savings contributions credit. Attach Form 8880.		34			
35	Child tax credit. Attach Schedule 8812, if required.		35			
36	Add lines 31 through 35. These are your total credits.			36		0
37	Subtract line 36 from line 30. If line 36 is more than line 30, enter -0-.			37		0
38	Health care: individual responsibility (see instructions). Full-year coverage ☒			38		
39	Add line 37 and line 38. This is your total tax.			39		0
40	Federal income tax withheld from Forms W-2 and 1099.	40	68			
41	2015 estimated tax payments and amount applied from 2014 return.	41				

If you have a qualifying child, attach Schedule EIC.

42a	Earned income credit (EIC).	42a	1,369			
b	Nontaxable combat pay election. 42b					
43	Additional child tax credit. Attach Schedule 8812.	43	152			
44	American opportunity credit from Form 8863, line 8.	44				
45	Net premium tax credit. Attach Form 8962.	45				
46	Add lines 40, 41, 42a, 43, 44, and 45. These are your total payments.		▶ 46		1,589	

Refund

47	If line 46 is more than line 39, subtract line 39 from line 46. This is the amount you overpaid.			47		1,589
48a	Amount of line 47 you want refunded to you. If Form 8888 is attached, check here ▶ ☐			48a		1,589

Direct deposit? See instructions and fill in 48b, 48c, and 48d or Form 8888.

▶ b	Routing number	[redacted]	▶ c Type: ☒ Checking ☐ Savings	
▶ d	Account number	[redacted]		

49	Amount of line 47 you want applied to your 2016 estimated tax.	49			

Amount you owe

50	Amount you owe. Subtract line 46 from line 39. For details on how to pay, see instructions.	▶ 50		
51	Estimated tax penalty (see instructions).	51		

Third party designee

Do you want to allow another person to discuss this return with the IRS (see instructions)? ☒ Yes. Complete the following. ☐ No

Designee's name ▶ HRB TAX GROUP INC Phone no. ▶ 559-324-8491 Personal identification number (PIN) ▶ 06374

Sign here

Under penalties of perjury, I declare that I have examined this return and accompanying schedules and statements, and to the best of my knowledge and belief, they are true, correct, and accurately list all amounts and sources of income I received during the tax year. Declaration of preparer (other than the taxpayer) is based on all information of which the preparer has any knowledge.

Joint return? See instructions. Keep a copy for your records.

Your signature	Date	Your occupation CARE GIVER	Daytime phone number
Spouse's signature. If a joint rtn., both must sign.	Date	Spouse's occupation	If the IRS sent you an Identity Protection PIN, enter it here (see inst.)

Paid preparer use only

Print/type preparer's name RENUKA JAYAKRISHNAN	Preparer's signature	Date 02-09-2016	Check ☐ if self-employed	PTIN P01277350
Firm's name ▶ HRB TAX GROUP INC			Firm's EIN ▶ 431871840	
Firm's address ▶ 1610 HERNDON AVE CLOVIS CA 93611			Phone no. 5593248491	

FDA 15 1040A2 DWF 1040 Form Software Copyright 1996 - 2016 HRB Tax Group, Inc. Form **1040A** (2015)

SCHEDULE EIC

(Form 1040A or 1040)

Department of the Treasury
Internal Revenue Service (99)

Earned Income Credit

Qualifying Child Information

▶ Complete and attach to Form 1040A or 1040 only if you have a qualifying child.
▶ Information about Schedule EIC (Form 1040A or 1040) and its instructions is at www.irs.gov/scheduleeic.

1040A
1040
EIC

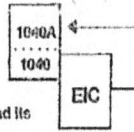

OMB No. 1545-0074

2015

Attachment
Sequence No. 43

Name(s) shown on return
█████████████

Your social security number
█████████████

Before you begin:

• See the instructions for Form 1040A, lines 42a and 42b, or Form 1040, lines 66a and 66b, to make sure that (a) you can take the EIC, and (b) you have a qualifying child.

• Be sure the child's name on line 1 and social security number (SSN) on line 2 agree with the child's social security card. Otherwise, at the time we process your return, we may reduce or disallow your EIC. If the name or SSN on the child's social security card is not correct, call the Social Security Administration at 1-800-772-1213.

! CAUTION

• You can't claim the EIC for a child who didn't live with you for more than half of the year.

• If you take the EIC even though you are not eligible, you may not be allowed to take the credit for up to 10 years. See the instructions for details.

• It will take us longer to process your return and issue your refund if you do not fill in all lines that apply for each qualifying child.

Qualifying Child Information	Child 1	Child 2	Child 3
1 Child's name If you have more than three qualifying children, you have to list only three to get the maximum credit.	First name Last name ████████	First name Last name	First name Last name
2 Child's SSN The child must have an SSN as defined in the instructions for Form 1040A, lines 42a and 42b, or Form 1040, lines 66a and 66b, unless the child was born and died in 2015. If your child was born and died in 2015 and did not have an SSN, enter "Died" on this line and attach a copy of the child's birth certificate, death certificate, or hospital medical records.	████████ CLIENT COPY		
3 Child's year of birth	Year __2015__ If born after 1996 **and** the child is younger than you (or your spouse, if filing jointly), skip lines 4a and 4b; go to line 5.	Year _____ If born after 1996 **and** the child is younger than you (or your spouse, if filing jointly), skip lines 4a and 4b; go to line 5.	Year _____ If born after 1996 **and** the child is younger than you (or your spouse, if filing jointly), skip lines 4a and 4b; go to line 5.
4a Was the child under age 24 at the end of 2015, a student, and younger than you (or your spouse, if filing jointly)?	☐ Yes. Go to line 5. ☐ No. Go to line 4b.	☐ Yes. Go to line 5. ☐ No. Go to line 4b.	☐ Yes. Go to line 5. ☐ No. Go to line 4b.
b Was the child permanently and totally disabled during any part of 2015?	☐ Yes. Go to line 5. ☐ No. The child is not a qualifying child.	☐ Yes. Go to line 5. ☐ No. The child is not a qualifying child.	☐ Yes. Go to line 5. ☐ No. The child is not a qualifying child.
5 Child's relationship to you (for example, son, daughter, grandchild, niece, nephew, foster child, etc.)	DAUGHTER		
6 Number of months child lived with you in the United States during 2015 ● If the child lived with you for more than half of 2015 but less than 7 months, enter "7." ● If the child was born or died in 2015 and your home was the child's home for more than half the time he or she was alive during 2015, enter "12."	__12__ months Do not enter more than 12 months.	_____ months Do not enter more than 12 months.	_____ months Do not enter more than 12 months.

For Paperwork Reduction Act Notice, see your tax return instructions.

Schedule EIC (Form 1040A or 1040) 2015

Child Tax Credit

▶ Attach to Form 1040, Form 1040A, or Form 1040NR.
▶ Information about Schedule 8812 and its separate instructions is at www.irs.gov/schedule8812.

OMB No. 1545-0074

1040A
1040NR
8812

2015

Attachment
Sequence No. 47

Name(s) shown on return

Your social security number

Part I Filers Who Have Certain Child Dependent(s) with an ITIN (Individual Taxpayer Identification Number)

! CAUTION Complete this part only for each dependent who has an ITIN and for whom you are claiming the child tax credit.
If your dependent is not a qualifying child for the credit, you cannot include that dependent in the calculation of this credit.

Answer the following questions for each dependent listed on Form 1040, line 6c; Form 1040A, line 6c; or Form 1040NR, line 7c, who has an ITIN (Individual Taxpayer Identification Number) and that you indicated is a qualifying child for the child tax credit by checking column (4) for that dependent.

A For the first dependent identified with an ITIN and listed as a qualifying child for the child tax credit, did this child meet the substantial presence test? See separate instructions.
☐ Yes   ☐ No

B For the second dependent identified with an ITIN and listed as a qualifying child for the child tax credit, did this child meet the substantial presence test? See separate instructions.
☐ Yes   ☐ No

C For the third dependent identified with an ITIN and listed as a qualifying child for the child tax credit, did this child meet the substantial presence test? See separate instructions.
☐ Yes   ☐ No

D For the fourth dependent identified with an ITIN and listed as a qualifying child for the child tax credit, did this child meet the substantial presence test? See separate instructions.
☐ Yes   ☐ No

CLIENT COPY

Note: If you have more than four dependents identified with an ITIN and listed as a qualifying child for the child tax credit, see separate instructions and check here ··· ▶ ☐

Part II Additional Child Tax Credit Filers

1 If you file Form 2555 or 2555-EZ stop here, you cannot claim the additional child tax credit.
If you are required to use the worksheet in Pub. 972, enter the amount from line 8 of the Child Tax Credit Worksheet in the publication. Otherwise:

1040 filers: Enter the amount from line 6 of your Child Tax Credit Worksheet (see the Instructions for Form 1040, line 52).

1040A filers: Enter the amount from line 6 of your Child Tax Credit Worksheet (see the Instructions for Form 1040A, line 35).

1040NR filers: Enter the amount from line 6 of your Child Tax Credit Worksheet (see the Instructions for Form 1040NR, line 49).

1		1,000

2 Enter the amount from Form 1040, line 52; Form 1040A, line 35; or Form 1040NR, line 49 ··············

2		0
3		1,000

3 Subtract line 2 from line 1. If zero, stop; you cannot take this credit ························

4a Earned income (see separate instructions) ························· | 4a | 4,011

b Nontaxable combat pay (see separate instr.) ··· 4b

5 Is the amount on line 4a more than $3,000?
☐ No.   Leave line 5 blank and enter -0- on line 6.
☒ Yes. Subtract $3,000 from the amount on line 4a. Enter the result ········ | 5 | 1,011

6 Multiply the amount on line 5 by 15% (.15) and enter the result ···························· | 6 | 152

Next. Do you have three or more qualifying children?
☒ No.   If line 6 is zero, stop; you cannot take this credit. Otherwise, skip Part III and enter the **smaller** of line 3 or line 6 on line 13.
☐ Yes. If line 6 is equal to or more than line 3, skip Part III and enter the amount from line 3 on line 13. Otherwise, go to line 7.

For Paperwork Reduction Act Notice, see your tax return instructions.   Schedule 8812 (Form 1040A or 1040) 2015

Part III Certain Filers Who Have Three or More Qualifying Children

7   Withheld social security, Medicare, and Additional Medicare taxes from
Form(s) W-2, boxes 4 and 6. If married filing jointly, include your spouse's
amounts with yours. If your employer withheld or you paid Additional
Medicare Tax or tier 1 RRTA taxes, see separate instructions · · · · · · · · · · · · · ·   **7**

8   1040 filers: Enter the total of the amounts from Form 1040, lines
27 and 58, plus any taxes that you identified using
code "UT" and entered on line 62.

1040A filers: Enter -0-.   **8**
1040NR filers: Enter the total of the amounts from Form 1040NR,
lines 27 and 56, plus any taxes that you identified using
code "UT" and entered on line 60.

9   Add lines 7 and 8 ·   **9**

10 1040 filers: Enter the total of the amounts from Form 1040, lines
66a and 71.

1040A filers: Enter the total of the amount from Form 1040A, line
42a, plus any excess social security and tier 1 RRTA
taxes withheld that you entered to the left of line 46   **10**
(see separate instructions).

1040NR filers: Enter the amount from Form 1040NR, line 67.

11 Subtract line 10 from line 9. If zero or less, enter -0- ·   **11**
12 Enter the **larger** of line 6 or line 11 ·   **12**
Next, enter the **smaller** of line 3 or line 12 on line 13.

Part IV Additional Child Tax Credit

13 This is your additional child tax credit ·   **13**   152

Enter this amount on
Form 1040, line 67,
Form 1040A, line 43, or
Form 1040NR, line 64.

| 1040 |
| 1040A |
| 1040NR |

CLIENT COPY

Form **8867**	Paid Preparer's Earned Income Credit Checklist	OMB No. 1545-1629
	▶ To be completed by preparer and filed with Form 1040, 1040A, or 1040EZ.	**2015**
Department of the Treasury Internal Revenue Service	▶ Information about Form 8867 and its separate instructions is at www.irs.gov/form8867.	Attachment Sequence No. 177

Taxpayer name(s) shown on return	Taxpayer's social security number
▓▓▓▓▓▓▓▓▓	607-22-1783

For the definitions of **Qualifying Child** and **Earned Income**, see Pub. 596.

Part I — All Taxpayers

1 Enter preparer's name and PTIN ▶ RENUKA JAYAKRISHNAN P01277350

2 Is the taxpayer's filing status married filing separately? . . . . ☐ Yes ☒ No

   ▶ If you checked **"Yes"** on line 2, **stop**; the taxpayer **cannot** take the EIC. Otherwise, continue.

3 Does the taxpayer (and the taxpayer's spouse if filing jointly) have a social security number (SSN)
that allows him or her to work and is valid for EIC purposes? See the instructions before answering . . . . ☒ Yes ☐ No

   ▶ If you checked **"No"** on line 3, **stop**; the taxpayer **cannot** take the EIC. Otherwise, continue.

4 Is the taxpayer (or the taxpayer's spouse if filing jointly) filing Form 2555 or Form 2555-EZ (relating to
the exclusion of foreign earned income)? . . . . ☐ Yes ☒ No

   ▶ If you checked **"Yes"** on line 4, **stop**; the taxpayer **cannot** take the EIC. Otherwise, continue.

5a Was the taxpayer (or the taxpayer's spouse) a nonresident alien for any part of 2015? . . . . ☐ Yes ☒ No

   ▶ If you checked **"Yes"** on line 5a, go to line 5b. Otherwise, skip line 5b and go to line 6.

b Is the taxpayer's filing status married filing jointly? . . . . CLIENT COPY ☐ Yes ☐ No

   ▶ If you checked **"Yes"** on line 5a and **"No"** on line 5b, **stop**; the taxpayer **cannot** take the EIC.
   Otherwise, continue.

6 Is the taxpayer's **investment income** more than $3,400? See the instructions before answering. . . . . ☐ Yes ☒ No

   ▶ If you checked **"Yes"** on line 6, **stop**; the taxpayer **cannot** take the EIC. Otherwise, continue.

7 Could the taxpayer be a **qualifying child** of another person for 2015? If the taxpayer's filing status is
married filing jointly, check **"No."** Otherwise, see instructions before answering . . . . ☐ Yes ☒ No

   ▶ If you checked **"Yes"** on line 7, **stop**; the taxpayer **cannot** take the EIC. Otherwise, go to
   Part II or Part III, whichever applies.

For Paperwork Reduction Act Notice, see separate instructions.   Form **8867** (2015)

FDA   15 88671   BWF 1040   Form Software Copyright 1996 - 2016 HRB Tax Group, Inc.

Part II Taxpayers With a Child

		Child 1	Child 2	Child 3
	Caution. If there is more than one child, complete lines 8 through 14 for one child before going to the next column.			
8	Child's name	[REDACTED]		
9	Is the child the taxpayer's son, daughter, stepchild, foster child, brother, sister, stepbrother, stepsister, half brother, half sister, or a descendant of any of them?	☒ Yes ☐ No	☐ Yes ☐ No	☐ Yes ☐ No
10	Was the child unmarried at the end of 2015? If the child was married at the end of 2015, see the instructions before answering	☒ Yes ☐ No	☐ Yes ☐ No	☐ Yes ☐ No
11	Did the child live with the taxpayer in the United States for over half of 2015? See the instructions before answering	☒ Yes ☐ No	☐ Yes ☐ No	☐ Yes ☐ No
12	Was the child (at the end of 2015)-- • Under age 19 and younger than the taxpayer (or the taxpayer's spouse, if the taxpayer files jointly), • Under age 24, a student (defined in the instructions), and younger than the taxpayer (or the taxpayer's spouse, if the taxpayer files jointly), or • Any age and permanently and totally disabled?	☒ Yes ☐ No	☐ Yes ☐ No	☐ Yes ☐ No

▶ If you checked "Yes" on lines 9, 10, 11, and 12, the child is the taxpayer's qualifying child; go to line 13a. If you checked "No" on line 9, 10, 11, or 12, the child is not the taxpayer's qualifying child; see the instructions for line 12.

| 13a | Do you or the taxpayer know of another person who could check "Yes" on lines 9, 10, 11, and 12 for the child? (If the only other person is the taxpayer's spouse, see the instructions before answering.) . . . . | ☐ Yes ☒ No | ☐ Yes ☐ No | ☐ Yes ☐ No |

▶ If you checked "No" on line 13a, go to line 14. Otherwise, go to line 13b.

| b | Enter the child's relationship to the other person(s) . . . . | | | |
| c | Under the tiebreaker rules, is the child treated as the taxpayer's qualifying child? See the instructions before answering . . . . | ☐ Yes ☐ No ☐ Don't know | ☐ Yes ☐ No ☐ Don't know | ☐ Yes ☐ No ☐ Don't know |

▶ If you checked "Yes" on line 13c, go to line 14. If you checked "No," the taxpayer cannot take the EIC based on this child and cannot take the EIC for taxpayers who do not have a qualifying child. If there is more than one child, see the Note at the bottom of this page. If you checked "Don't know," explain to the taxpayer that, under the tiebreaker rules, the taxpayer's EIC and other tax benefits may be disallowed. Then, if the taxpayer wants to take the EIC based on this child, complete lines 14 and 15. If not, and there are no other qualifying children, the taxpayer cannot take the EIC, including the EIC for taxpayers without a qualifying child; do not complete Part III. If there is more than one child, see the Note at the bottom of this page.

| 14 | Does the qualifying child have an SSN that allows him or her to work and is valid for EIC purposes? See the instructions before answering . . . . | ☒ Yes ☐ No | ☐ Yes ☐ No | ☐ Yes ☐ No |

▶ If you checked "No" on line 14, the taxpayer cannot take the EIC based on this child and cannot take the EIC available to taxpayers without a qualifying child. If there is more than one child, see the Note at the bottom of this page. If you checked "Yes" on line 14, continue.

| 15 | Are the taxpayer's earned income and adjusted gross income each less than the limit that applies to the taxpayer for 2015? See instructions . . . . | ☒ Yes ☐ No |

▶ If you checked "No" on line 15, stop; the taxpayer cannot take the EIC. If you checked "Yes" on line 15, the taxpayer can take the EIC. Complete Schedule EIC and attach it to the taxpayer's return. If there are two or three qualifying children with valid SSNs, list them on Schedule EIC in the same order as they are listed here. If the taxpayer's EIC was reduced or disallowed for a year after 1996, see Pub. 596 to see if Form 8862 must be filed. Go to line 20.

Note. If there is more than one child, complete lines 8 through 14 for the other child(ren) (but for no more than three qualifying children).

Form 8867 (2015)

Part III   Taxpayers Without a Qualifying Child

16 Was the taxpayer's main home, and the main home of the taxpayer's spouse if filing jointly, in the United States
for more than half the year? (Military personnel on extended active duty outside the United States are considered
to be living in the United States during that duty period.) See the instructions below answering .... ☐ Yes ☐ No

   ▶ If you checked "No" on line 16, stop; the taxpayer cannot take the EIC. Otherwise, continue.

17 Was the taxpayer, or the taxpayer's spouse if filing jointly, at least age 25 but under age 65 at the end of 2015?
See the instructions before answering .... ☐ Yes ☐ No

   ▶ If you checked "No" on line 17, stop; the taxpayer cannot take the EIC. Otherwise, continue.

18 Is the taxpayer eligible to be claimed as a dependent on anyone else's federal income tax return for 2015?
If the taxpayer's filing status is married filing jointly, check "No"........................... ☐ Yes ☐ No

   ▶ If you checked "Yes" on line 18, stop; the taxpayer cannot take the EIC. Otherwise, continue.

19 Are the taxpayer's earned income and adjusted gross income each less than the limit that applies to the
taxpayer for 2015? See instructions .... ☐ Yes ☐ No

   ▶ If you checked "No" on line 19, stop; the taxpayer cannot take the EIC. If you checked
"Yes" on line 19, the taxpayer can take the EIC. If the taxpayer's EIC was reduced or disallowed
for a year after 1996, see Pub. 596 to find out if **Form 8862** must be filed. Go to line 20.

Part IV   Due Diligence Requirements

20 Did you complete Form 8867 based on current information provided by the taxpayer or reasonably obtained
by you? .... ☒ Yes ☐ No

21 Did you complete the EIC worksheet found in the Form 1040, 1040A, or 1040EZ instructions (or your
own worksheet that provides the same information as the 1040, 1040A, or 1040EZ worksheet)? .... ☒ Yes ☐ No

22 If any qualifying child was not the taxpayer's son or daughter, do you know or did you ask why the
parents were not claiming the child? .... ☐ Yes ☐ No ☒ Does not apply

23 If the answer to question 13a is "Yes" (indicating that the child lived for more than half the year with
someone else who could claim the child for the EIC), did you explain the tiebreaker rules and
possible consequences of another person claiming your client's qualifying child? .... ☒ Yes ☐ No ☐ Does not apply

24 Did you ask this taxpayer any additional questions that are necessary to meet your knowledge
requirement? See the instructions before answering .... ☒ Yes ☐ No ☐ Does not apply

**To comply with the EIC knowledge requirement, you must not know or have reason to know
that any information used to determine the taxpayer's eligibility for, and the amount of, the
EIC is incorrect. You may not ignore the implications of information furnished to you or known by
you, and you must make reasonable inquiries if the information furnished to you appears to be
incorrect, inconsistent, or incomplete. At the time you make these inquiries, you must
document in your files the inquiries you made and the taxpayer's responses.**

25 Did you document (a) the taxpayer's answer to question 22 (if applicable), (b) whether you explained
the tiebreaker rules to the taxpayer and any additional information you got from the taxpayer as a
result, and (c) any additional questions you asked and the taxpayer's answers? .... ☒ Yes ☐ No ☐ Does not apply

▶ You have complied with all the due diligence requirements if you:
  1. Completed the actions described on lines 20 and 21 and checked "Yes" on those lines,
  2. Completed the actions described on lines 22, 23, 24, and 25 (if they apply) and checked "Yes" (or
    "Does not apply") on those lines,
  3. Submit Form 8867 in the manner required, and
  4. Keep all five of the following records for 3 years from the latest of the dates specified in the
    instructions under Document Retention:

    a. Form 8867,
    b. The EIC worksheet(s) or your own worksheet(s),
    c. Copies of any taxpayer documents you relied on to determine eligibility for or amount of EIC,
    d. A record of how, when, and from whom the information used to prepare the form and
      worksheet(s) was obtained, and
    e. A record of any additional questions you asked and your client's answers.

▶ You have not complied with all the due diligence requirements if you checked "No" on line 20, 21, 22,
23, 24, or 25. You may have to pay a $505 penalty for each failure to comply.

Part V   Documents Provided to You

26   Identify below any document that the taxpayer provided to you and that you relied on to determine the taxpayer's EIC
     eligibility. Check all that apply. **Keep a copy of any documents you relied on.** See the instructions before answering.
     If there is no qualifying child, check box a. If there is no disabled child, check box o.

Residency of Qualifying Child(ren)	
☐ a No qualifying child	☐ i Place of worship statement
☐ b School records or statement	☐ j Indian tribal official statement
☐ c Landlord or property management statement	☐ k Employer statement
☐ d Health care provider statement	☐ l Other (specify) ▼
☐ e Medical records	
☐ f Child care provider records	
☐ g Placement agency statement	
☐ h Social service records or statement	☐ m Did not rely on any documents, but made notes in file
	☒ n Did not rely on any documents

Disability of Qualifying Child(ren)	
☒ o No disabled child	☐ s Other (specify) ▼
☐ p Doctor statement	
☐ q Other health care provider statement	
☐ r Social services agency or program statement	☐ t Did not rely on any documents, but made notes in file
	☐ u Did not rely on any documents

27   If a Schedule C is included with this return, identify below the information that the taxpayer provided to you and that you relied
     on to prepare the Schedule C. Check all that apply. **Keep a copy of any documents you relied on.** See the instructions
     before answering. If there is no Schedule C, check box a.

Documents or Other Information	
☒ a No Schedule C	☐ h Bank statements
☐ b Business license	☐ i Reconstruction of income and expenses
☐ c Forms 1099	☐ j Other (specify) ▼
☐ d Records of gross receipts provided by taxpayer	
☐ e Taxpayer summary of income	
☐ f Records of expenses provided by taxpayer	☐ k Did not rely on any documents, but made notes in file
☐ g Taxpayer summary of expenses	☐ l Did not rely on any documents

FDA   15   88674   BWF 1040   Form Software Copyright 1996 – 2016 HRB Tax Group, Inc.   Form **8867** (2015)

Form 8879

Department of the Treasury
Internal Revenue Service

..S e-file Signature Authoriza..on

▶ Do not send to the IRS.This is not a tax return.
▶ Keep this form for your records.
▶ Information about Form 8879 and its instructions is at www.irs.gov/form8879.

CLIENT COPY

2015

Submission Identification Number (SID) ▶

Taxpayer's name	Social security number
Spouse's name	Spouse's social security number

Part I Tax Return Information — Tax Year Ending December 31, 2015 (Whole Dollars Only)

1	Adjusted gross income (Form 1040, line 38; Form 1040A, line 22; Form 1040EZ, line 4)	1	5,376
2	Total tax (Form 1040, line 63; Form 1040A, line 39; Form 1040EZ, line 12)	2	
3	Federal income tax withheld (Form 1040, line 64; Form 1040A, line 40; Form 1040EZ, line 7)	3	68
4	Refund (Form 1040, line 76a; Form 1040A, line 48a; Form 1040EZ, line 13a; Form 1040-SS, Part I, line 13a)	4	1,589
5	Amount you owe (Form 1040, line 78; Form 1040A, line 50; Form 1040EZ, line 14)	5	

Part II Taxpayer Declaration and Signature Authorization (Be sure you get and keep a copy of your return)

Under penalties of perjury, I declare that I have examined a copy of my electronic individual income tax return and accompanying schedules and statements for the tax year ending December 31, 2015, and to the best of my knowledge and belief, it is true, correct, and complete. I further declare that the amounts in Part I above are the amounts from my electronic income tax return. I consent to allow my intermediate service provider, transmitter, or electronic return originator (ERO) to send my return to the IRS and to receive from the IRS (a) an acknowledgment of receipt or reason for rejection of the transmission, (b) the reason for any delay in processing the return or refund, and (c) the date of any refund. If applicable, I authorize the U.S. Treasury and its designated Financial Agent to initiate an ACH electronic funds withdrawal (direct debit) entry to the financial institution account indicated in the tax preparation software for payment of my federal taxes owed on this return and/or a payment of estimated tax, and the financial institution to debit the entry to this account. This authorization is to remain in full force and effect until I notify the U.S. Treasury Financial Agent to terminate the authorization. To revoke (cancel) a payment, I must contact the U.S. Treasury Financial Agent at 1-888-353-4537. Payment cancellation requests must be received no later than 2 business days prior to the payment (settlement) date. I also authorize the financial institutions involved in the processing of the electronic payment of taxes to receive confidential information necessary to answer inquiries and resolve issues related to the payment. I further acknowledge that the personal identification number (PIN) below is my signature for my electronic income tax return and, if applicable, my Electronic Funds Withdrawal Consent.

Taxpayer's PIN: check one box only

[X] I authorize **HRB TAX GROUP INC** ~~CLIENT COPY~~ to enter or generate my PIN | 11783
ERO firm name | Enter five digits, but do not enter all zeros

as my signature on my tax year 2015 electronically filed income tax return.

[ ] I will enter my PIN as my signature on my tax year 2015 electronically filed income tax return. Check this box only if you are entering your own PIN and your return is filed using the Practitioner PIN method. The ERO must complete Part III below.

Your signature ▶ **Signature and Date on file**   Date ▶ _____

Spouse's PIN: check one box only

[ ] I authorize _____ to enter or generate my PIN |
ERO firm name | Enter five digits, but do not enter all zeros

as my signature on my tax year 2015 electronically filed income tax return.

[ ] I will enter my PIN as my signature on my tax year 2015 electronically filed income tax return. Check this box only if you are entering your own PIN and your return is filed using the Practitioner PIN method. The ERO must complete Part III below.

Spouse's signature ▶ **Signature and Date on file**   Date ▶ _____

Practitioner PIN Method Returns Only — continue below

Part III Certification and Authentication — Practitioner PIN Method Only

ERO's EFIN/PIN. Enter your six-digit EFIN followed by your five-digit self-selected PIN. | 77178335624
| Do not enter all zeros

I certify that the above numeric entry is my PIN, which is my signature for the tax year 2015 electronically filed income tax return for the taxpayer(s) indicated above. I confirm that I am submitting this return in accordance with the requirements of the Practitioner PIN method and **Publication 1345,** Handbook for Authorized IRS e-file Providers of Individual Income Tax Returns.

ERO's signature ▶ _____   Date ▶ 02-09-2016

ERO Must Retain This Form — See Instructions
Do Not Submit This Form to the IRS Unless Requested To Do So

For Paperwork Reduction Act Notice, see your tax return instructions.

Form **8879** (2015)

FDA   Form Software Copyright 1996 - 2016 HRB Tax Group, Inc.   C1111D   16_8879CC

94 | Page

TAXABLE YEAR
2015 **California Resident Income Tax Return**

FORM
540

APE

~~ATTACH FEDERAL RETURN~~

15

A
R
RP

CA 93611

APT 161

01-26-1979

Filing Status	1 ☒ Single	4 ☐ Head of household (with qualifying person). See instructions.
	2 ☐ Married/RDP filing jointly. See inst.	5 ☐ Qualifying widow(er) with dependent child. Enter year spouse/RDP died
	3 ☐ Married/RDP filing separately. Enter spouse's/RDP's SSN or ITIN above and full name here	

NOT AVAILABLE YET
DO NOT PAPER FILE
CLIENT COPY

If your California filing status is different from your federal filing status, check the box here . . . . ● ☐

6 If someone can claim you (or your spouse/RDP) as a dependent, check the box here. See inst. . . ● 6 ☐

► For line 7, line 8, line 9, and line 10: Multiply the amount you enter in the box by the pre-printed dollar amount for that line.

Whole dollars only

7 Personal: If you checked box 1, 3, or 4 above, enter 1 in the box. If you checked
box 2 or 5, enter 2, in the box. If you checked the box on line 6, see instructions ○ 7 |1| X $109 = ○ $ | 109.|

8 Blind: If you (or your spouse/RDP) are visually impaired, enter 1;
if both are visually impaired, enter 2 . . . . ● 8 ☐ X $109 = ○ $ | |

9 Senior: If you (or your spouse/RDP) are 65 or older, enter 1;
if both are 65 or older, enter 2 . . . . ● 9 ☐ X $109 = ● $ | |

10 Dependents: Do not include yourself or your spouse/RDP.

	Dependent 1	Dependent 2	Dependent 3
First name	◉	◉	◉
Last name	◉	◉	◉
SSN	●	●	●
Dependent's relationship to you	◉ DAUGHTER	◉	◉

Total dependent exemptions . . . . ● 10 |1| X $337 = ◉ $ | 337.|

11 Exemption amount: Add line 7 through line 10. Transfer this amount to line 32 . . . . ◉ 11 $ | 446.|

---

195 | 3101154

Form 540 C1 2015 Side 1

Your name: ▮▮▮▮▮▮▮▮▮▮▮▮   Your SSN or ITIN: ▮▮▮▮▮▮▮▮▮▮

Taxable Income

12 State wages from your Form(s) W-2, box 16 .... ● 12 | 4,011.

13 Enter federal adjusted gross income from Form 1040, line 37; 1040A, line 21; or 1040EZ, line 4 ..... ◉ 13 | 5,376.

14 California adjustments – subtractions. Enter the amount from Schedule CA (540), line 37, column B .● 14 | 1,365.

15 Subtract line 14 from line 13. If less than zero, enter the result in parentheses. See instructions ...... 15 | 4,011.

16 California adjustments – additions. Enter the amount from Schedule CA (540), line 37, column C ...● 16 |

17 California adjusted gross income. Combine line 15 and line 16 .... ● 17 | 4,011.

18 Enter the larger of: { Your California **itemized deductions** from Schedule CA (540), line 44; OR
Your California **standard deduction** shown below for your filing status:
● Single or Married/RDP filing separately $4,044
● Married/RDP filing jointly, Head of household, or Qualifying widow(er) $8,088
If Married/RDP filing separately or the box on line 6 is checked, STOP. See instructions } ● 18 | 4,044.

19 Subtract line 18 from line 17. This is your **taxable income**. If less than zero, enter -0- .... ◉ 19 | 0.

Tax

31 Tax. Check the box if from: ☒ Tax Table ☐ Tax Rate Schedule
● ☐ FTB 3800 ● ☐ FTB 3803 .... ● 31

NOT AVAILABLE YET
DO NOT PAPER FILE
CLIENT COPY

32 Exemption credits. Enter the amount from line 11. If your federal AGI is more than $178,706,
see instructions .... ● 32 | 446.

33 Subtract line 32 from line 31. If less than zero, enter -0- .... ◉ 33 |

34 Tax. See instructions. Check the box if from: ● ☐ Schedule G-1 ● ☐ FTB 5870A ● 34 | 0.

35 Add line 33 and line 34 .... ● 35

Special Credits

40 Nonrefundable Child and Dependent Care Expenses Credit. See instructions .... ● 40 |

43 Enter credit name [   ] code ● [ ] and amount ...... ● 43 |

44 Enter credit name [   ] code ● [ ] and amount ...... ● 44 |

45 To claim more than two credits, see instructions. Attach Schedule P (540) .... ● 45 |

46 Nonrefundable renter's credit. See instructions .... ● 46 |

47 Add line 40 through line 46. These are your total credits .... ◉ 47 |

48 Subtract line 47 from line 35. If less than zero, enter -0- .... ◉ 48 |

Other Taxes

61 Alternative minimum tax. Attach Schedule P (540) .... ● 61 |

62 Mental Health Services Tax. See instructions .... ● 62 |

63 Other taxes and credit recapture. See instructions .... ● 63 |

64 Add line 48, line 61, line 62, and line 63. This is your total tax .... ● 64 |

CA Form 540 C1 (2015)

Your name: [REDACTED]　　　　　　　Your SSN or ITIN: [REDACTED]

Payments

71 California income tax withheld. See instructions .... ● 71 [ ]

72 2015 CA estimated tax and other payments. See instructions .... ● 72 [ ]

73 Withholding (Form 592-B and/or 593). See instructions .... ● 73 [ ]

74 Excess SDI (or VPDI) withheld. See instructions .... ● 74 [ ]

75 Earned Income Tax Credit (EITC) .... ● 75 [1,163.]

76 Add lines 71 through 75. These are your total payments. See instructions .... ◉ 76 [1,163.]

Use Tax

91 Use Tax. **This is not a total line.** See instructions .... ● [ ]

Overpaid Tax/ Tax Due

92 **Payments balance.** If line 76 is more than line 91, subtract line 91 from line 76 .... ○ 92 [1,163.]

93 **Use Tax balance.** If line 91 is more than line 76, subtract line 76 from line 91 .... ○ 93 [ ]

94 Overpaid tax. If line 92 is more than line 64, subtract line 64 from line 92 .... ◉ 94 [1,163.]

95 Amount of line 94 you want applied to your 2016 estimated tax .... ● 95 [ ]

96 Overpaid tax available this year. Subtract line 95 from line 94 .... ● 96 [1,163.]

97 **Tax due.** If line 92 is less than line 64, subtract line 92 from line 64 .... ◉ 97 [ ]

NOT AVAILABLE YET
DO NOT PAPER FILE
CLIENT COPY

| | 195 | 3103154 | | Form 540 C1 2015 **Side 3** |

Form Software Copyright 1998 - 2016 HRB Tax Group, Inc.

CA Form 540 C1 (2015)

Your name: [REDACTED] Your SSN or ITIN: [REDACTED]

	Code	Amount
California Seniors Special Fund. See instructions	● 400	
Alzheimer's Disease/Related Disorders Fund	● 401	
Rare and Endangered Species Preservation Program	● 403	
California Breast Cancer Research Fund	● 405	
California Firefighters' Memorial Fund	● 406	
Emergency Food for Families Fund	● 407	
California Peace Officer Memorial Foundation Fund	● 408	
California Sea Otter Fund	● 410	
California Cancer Research Fund	● 413	
Child Victims of Human Trafficking Fund	● 419	
School Supplies for Homeless Children Fund	● 422	
State Parks Protection Fund/Parks Pass Purchase	● 423	
Protect Our Coast and Oceans Fund	● 424	
Keep Arts in Schools Fund	● 425	
California Senior Legislature Fund	● 427	
Habitat for Humanity Fund	● 428	
California Sexual Violence Victim Services Fund	● 429	
State Children's Trust Fund for the Prevention of Child Abuse	● 430	
Prevention of Animal Homelessness & Cruelty Fund	● 431	
110 Add code 400 through code 429. This is your total contribution	● 110	0.

NOT AVAILABLE YET
DO NOT PAPER FILE
CLIENT COPY

BWF
CA Form 540 C1 (2015)

Your name: [redacted]   Your SSN or ITIN: [redacted]

Amount You Owe

111   AMOUNT YOU OWE. If you do not have an amount on line 96, add line 93, line 97, and line 110. See instructions.   **Do not send cash.**
      Mail to: FRANCHISE TAX BOARD
               PO BOX 942867
               SACRAMENTO CA 94267-0001 .... ●111 [   ]

      Pay online — Go to ftb.ca.gov for more information.

Interest and Penalties

112   Interest, late return penalties, and late payment penalties .... 112 [   ]

113   Underpayment of estimated tax. Check the box: ● ☐ FTB 5805 attached ● ☐ FTB 5805F attached.. ●113 [   ]

114   Total amount due. See instructions. Enclose, but do not staple, any payment .... 114 [   ]

Refund and Direct Deposit

115   REFUND OR NO AMOUNT DUE. Subtract the sum of line 110, line 112 and line 113 from line 96. See instructions.
      Mail to: FRANCHISE TAX BOARD
               PO BOX 942840
               SACRAMENTO CA 94240-0001 .... ●115 [1,163.   ]

      Fill in the information to authorize direct deposit of your refund into one or two accounts. Do not attach a voided check or a deposit slip.
      See instructions.

      Have you verified the routing and account numbers? Use whole dollars only.

      All or the following amount of my refund (line 115) is authorized for direct deposit into the account shown below.

      NOT AVAILABLE YET
      DO NOT PAPER FILE
      CLIENT COPY

                                            ● Type
      ● Routing number   ☐ Checking ● Account number   ●116 Direct deposit amount
      [   ]   ☐ Savings   [   ]   [   ]

      The remaining amount of my refund (line 115) is authorized for direct deposit into the account shown below.

                                            ● Type
      ● Routing number   ☐ Checking ● Account number   ●117 Direct deposit amount
      [   ]   ☐ Savings   [   ]   [   ]

IMPORTANT: See the instructions to find out if you should attach a copy of your complete federal tax return.

To learn about your privacy rights, how we may use your information, and the consequences for not providing the requested information, go to **ftb.ca.gov** and search for **privacy notice.** To request this notice by mail, call 800.852.5711. Under penalties of perjury, I declare that I have examined this tax return, including accompanying schedules and statements, and to the best of my knowledge and belief, it is true, correct, and complete.

Your signature   Date   Spouse's/RDP's signature (if a joint tax return, both must sign)
X   X

Sign Here

It is unlawful to forge a spouse's/RDP's signature.
Joint tax return? (See instructions)

Your email address (optional). Enter only one email address.   Daytime phone number (optional)
[redacted]   [redacted]

Paid preparer's signature (declaration of preparer is based on all information of which preparer has any knowledge)
[   ]

Firm's name (or yours, if self-employed)   ●PTIN
HRB TAX GROUP INC   P01277350
Firm's address 1610 HERNDON AVE   ●FEIN
CLOVIS CA 93611   431871840

Do you want to allow another person to discuss this tax return with us? See instructions .... ● ☒ Yes ☐ No

Print Third Party Designee's Name   Telephone Number
RENUKA JAYAKRISHNAN   559-324-8491

                        195   3105154   Form 540 C1 2015 Side 5
                                                      Form Software Copyright 1998 - 2016 HRB Tax Group, Inc.

California Adjustments --- Residents

SCHEDULE
CA (540)

Important: Attach this schedule behind Form 540, Side 5 as a supporting California schedule.

Name(s) as shown on tax return

SSN or ITIN
607-22-1783

Part I Income Adjustment Schedule
Section A – Income

	A Federal Amounts (taxable amounts from your federal tax return)	B Subtractions See Instructions	C Additions See Instructions
7 Wages, salaries, tips, etc. See instructions before making an entry in column B or C 7	4011.		
8 Taxable Interest (b) .... 8(a)			
9 Ordinary dividends. See instructions. (b) ...... 9(a)			
10 Taxable refunds, credits, offsets of state and local income taxes 10			
11 Alimony received 11			
12 Business income or (loss) 12			
13 Capital gain or (loss). See instructions 13			
14 Other gains or (losses) 14			
15 IRA distributions. See instructions. (a) _____ 15(b)			
16 Pensions and annuities. See instructions. (a) _____ 16(b)			
17 Rental real estate, royalties, partnerships, S corporations, trusts, etc 17			
18 Farm income or (loss) 18			
19 Unemployment compensation 19	1365.	1365.	
20 Social security benefits (a) ⊙ _____ .... 20(b)			
21 Other income.			
a California lottery winnings e NOL from FTB 3805D,3805Z,		a	a
b Disaster loss deduction from FTB 3805V 3806, 3807, or 3809 21		b	b
c Federal NOL (Form 1040, line 21) f Other (describe)		c	c ⊙
d NOL deduction from FTB 3805V ⊙			
22 Total. Combine line 7 through line 21 in column A. Add line 7 through line 21 in column B and column C. Go to Section B. 22	5376.	1365.	1365. ⊙

Section B – Adjustments to Income

	A	B	C
23 Educator expenses 23			
24 Certain business expenses of reservists, performing artists, and fee-basis government officials...................... 24			
25 Health savings account deduction 25			
26 Moving expenses........................ 26			
27 Deductible part of self-employment tax 27			
28 Self-employed SEP, SIMPLE, and qualified plans 28			
29 Self-employed health insurance deduction 29			
30 Penalty on early withdrawal of savings 30			
31a Alimony paid. (b) Recipient's: SSN ⊙			
Last name ⊙ _____ ... 31a			
32 IRA deduction 32			
33 Student loan interest deduction 33			
34 Tuition and fees 34			
35 Domestic production activities deduction.................. 35			
36 Add line 23 through line 31a and line 32 through line 35 in columns A, B, and C. See instructions 36			
37 Total. Subtract line 36 from line 22 in columns A, B, and C. See instructions........................ 37	5376.	1365.	

NOT AVAILABLE YET
DO NOT PAPER FILE
CLIENT COPY

UNLAYAO

BWF CA Schedule CA (540) (2015)

Part II Adjustments to Federal Itemized Deductions

38 Federal itemized deductions. Enter the amount from federal Schedule A (Form 1040), lines 4, 9, 15, 19, 20, 27,
and 28 .... ⊛ 38 ☐

39 Enter total of federal Schedule A (Form 1040), line 5 (State Disability Insurance, and state and local income tax, or
General Sales Tax) and line 8 (foreign income taxes only). See instructions .... ⊛ 39 ☐

40 Subtract line 39 from line 38 .... ⊛ 40 ☐

41 Other adjustments including California lottery losses. See instructions. Specify [   ] ...... ⊛ 41 ☐

42 Combine line 40 and line 41 .... ⊛ 42 ☐

43 Is your federal AGI (Form 540, line 13) more than the amount shown below for your filing status?

　　　Single or married/RDP filing separately $178,706
　　　Head of household $268,063
　　　Married/RDP filing jointly or qualifying widow(er) $357,417

　　No. Transfer the amount on line 42 to line 43.
　　Yes. Complete the Itemized Deductions Worksheet in the instructions for Schedule CA (540), line 43 .... ⊛ 43 ☐

44 Enter the larger of the amount on line 43 or your standard deduction listed below

　　　Single or married/RDP filing separately. See instructions $4,044
　　　Married/RDP filing jointly, head of household, or qualifying widow(er) $8,088

　　Transfer the amount on line 44 to Form 540, line 18 .... ⊛ 44 | 4044.

Side 2   Schedule CA (540) 2015   195   7732154

2015 CALIFORNIA DEPENDENT CONTINUATION

Dependent's Name	Birth Year	Dependent Social Security Number	Relationship to Taxpayer	Number of Months in Home
▓▓▓▓▓▓▓▓▓	2015	▓▓▓▓▓▓	DAUGHTER	12

NOT AVAILABLE YET
DO NOT PAPER FILE
CLIENT COPY

BWF 195

Date Accepted

TAXABLE YEAR		FORM
2015	California e-file Return Authorization for Individuals	8453

Your first name and initial	Last name	Suffix	Your SSN or ITIN
▇▇▇	▇▇▇		▇▇▇
If joint return, spouse's/RDP's first name and initial	Last name	Suffix	Spouse's/RDP's SSN or ITIN
Street address (number and street) or PO Box	Apt. no./Ste. no.	PMB/Private mailbox	Daytime telephone number
▇▇▇	▇▇▇		▇▇▇
City		State CA	ZIP Code 93611
▇▇▇			
Foreign country name	Foreign province/state/country		Foreign postal code

Part I   Tax Return Information (whole dollars only)

1 California adjusted gross income. (Form 540, line 17; Form 540 2EZ, line 16; Long Form 540NR, line 32; or Short Form 540NR, line 32) 1		4,011.
2 Refund or no amount due. (Form 540, line 115; Form 540 2EZ, line 32; Long Form 540NR, line 125; or Short Form 540NR, line 125) 2		1,163.
3 Amount you owe. (Form 540, line 111; Form 540 2EZ, line 31; Long Form 540NR, line 121; or Short Form 540NR, line 121) 3		0.

Part II   Settle Your Account Electronically for Taxable Year 2015 (Payment due 04/18/2016)

4	☐ Direct deposit of refund	5	☐ Electronic funds withdrawal	5a Amount		5b Withdrawal date (mm/dd/yyyy)

Part III   Make Estimated Tax Payments for Taxable Year 2016 These are NOT installment payments for the current amount you owe.

	First Payment Due 4/18/2016	Second Payment Due 6/15/2016	Third Payment Due 9/15/2016	Fourth Payment Due 1/17/2017
6 Amount				
7 Withdrawal date				

Part IV   Banking Information (Have you verified your banking information?)

8 Amount of ref. to be directly deposited to account below		12 ~~NOT AVAILABLE YET~~
9 Routing number		13 Routing number
10 Account number		14 Account number
11 Type of account: ☐ Checking ☐ Savings		15 ~~DO NOT PAPER FILE~~ Type of account ☐ Checking ☐ Savings

Part V   Declaration of Taxpayer(s)

I authorize my account to be settled as designated in Part II. If I check Part II, Box 4, I declare that the direct deposit refund information in Part IV agrees with the authorization stated on my return. If I check Part II, Box 5, I authorize an electronic funds withdrawal for the amount listed on line 5a and any estimated payment amounts listed on line 6 from the account listed on lines 9, 10, and 11. If I have filed a joint return, this is an irrevocable appointment of the other spouse/RDP as an agent to receive the refund or authorize an electronic funds withdrawal.

Under penalties of perjury, I declare that the information I provided to my electronic return originator (ERO), transmitter, or intermediate service provider, including my name, address, and social security number (SSN) or individual taxpayer identification number (ITIN), and the amounts shown in Part I above agrees with the information and amounts shown on the corresponding lines of my 2015 California income tax return. To the best of my knowledge and belief, my return is true, correct, and complete. If I am filing a balance due return, I understand that if the Franchise Tax Board (FTB) does not receive full and timely payment of my tax liability, I remain liable for the tax liability and all applicable interest and penalties. I authorize my return and accompanying schedules and statements be transmitted to the FTB by my ERO, transmitter, or intermediate service provider. **If the processing of my return or refund is delayed, I authorize the FTB to disclose to my ERO or intermediate service provider, the reason(s) for the delay or the date when the refund was sent.**

Sign Here	► Your signature	Date	► Spouse's/RDP's signature. If filing jointly, both must sign. It is unlawful to forge a spouse's/RDP's signature.	Date

Part VI   Declaration of Electronic Return Originator (ERO) and Paid Preparer. See instructions.

I declare that I have reviewed the above taxpayer's return and that the entries on form FTB 8453 are complete and correct to the best of my knowledge. (If I am only an intermediate service provider, I understand that I am not responsible for reviewing the taxpayer's return. I declare, however, that form FTB 8453 accurately reflects the data on the return.) I have obtained the taxpayer's signature on form FTB 8453 before transmitting this return to the FTB; I have provided the taxpayer with a copy of all forms and information that I will file with the FTB, and I have followed all other requirements described in FTB Pub. 1345, 2015 e-file Handbook for Authorized e-file Providers. I will keep form FTB 8453 on file for **four** years from the due date of the return or **four** years from the date the return is filed, whichever is later, and I will make a copy available to the FTB upon request. If I am also the paid preparer, under penalties of perjury, I declare that I have examined the above taxpayer's return and accompanying schedules and statements, and to the best of my knowledge and belief, they are true, correct, and complete. I make this declaration based on all information of which I have knowledge.

ERO Must Sign	ERO's signature ►	Date 02-09-2016	Check if also paid preparer ☒	Check if self-employed ☐	ERO's PTIN P01277350
	Firm's name (or yours if self-employed) and address ►	HRB TAX GROUP INC 1610 HERNDON AVE CLOVIS CA		FEIN 431871840	ZIP Code 93611

Under penalties of perjury, I declare that I have examined the above taxpayer's return and accompanying schedules and statements, and to the best of my knowledge and belief, they are true, correct, and complete. I make this declaration based on all information of which I have knowledge.

Paid Preparer Must Sign	Paid preparer's signature ►	Date 02-09-2016	Check if self-employed ☐	Paid preparer's PTIN P01277350
	Firm's name (or yours if self-employed) and address ►		FEIN	ZIP Code

For Privacy Notice, get FTB 1131 ENG/SP.

FTB 8453 2015

D5

EXHIBIT '19'

Witness List

WITNESS LIST

If necessary, the following individual(s) will provide testimony in support of Respondent's applications for relief from removal:

1. Name: ███████████████
   Summary of Testimony: Respondent's mother will provide testimony regarding her relationship with Respondent, Respondent's struggles, rehabilitation and good moral character and the effect that Respondent's deportation would have on their entire family.
   Alien Number: USC
   Length of Testimony: 20 Minutes
   Language: English

2. Name: ████████ - Sister
   Summary of Testimony: Respondent's sister will provide testimony regarding her relationship with Respondent, Respondent's struggles, rehabilitation and good moral character and the effect that Respondent's deportation would have on their entire family.
   Alien Number: USC
   Length of Testimony: 20 Minutes
   Language: English

3. Name: ████████ - Friend
   Summary of Testimony: Respondent's friend will provide testimony regarding her friendship with Respondent and Respondent's good moral character.
   Alien Number: USC
   Length of Testimony: 10 Minutes
   Language: English

EXHIBIT '20'

Criminal History Chart

CRIMINAL HISTORY CHART

Date & Docket No.	Conviction	Sentence
07/24/2007 F07904397	CPC § 484E(d) – Misd Credit/Debit Card Fraud	36 Months Probation 3 Days Jail
12/29/2008 F08902017	CHSC § 11377(a) – Felony Possession of Controlled Substance	24 Months Probation 2 Days Jail
12/29/2008 F08907500	CHSC § 11377(a) – Felony Possession of Controlled Substance	24 Months Probation 1 Day Jail

EXHIBIT '21'

Letter from Respondent's Sister

May 15, 2016

Immigration Status: United States of America Natural Born Citizen

████████████████

Hanford, CA. 93230

████████████

Relationship: Sister

Occupation: Dual-rate Supervisor, Table Games

Dear Immigration Judge,

    I am ███████████████ the sister of ██████████████. She has been a part of my life for as long as I could remember. She's the mother to my niece ████ who will be turning 1 on July 11th, 2016.

    Like any normal sibling relationship, we have had our ups and downs. My sister has always been a huge part in my decision making. She doesn't know it, nor do I ever tell her, ███████████, is also my daughter Ava's godmother. I wish you could see how they are when they are around each other, you would think that they had their own language, laughing and giggling, it makes my heart melt. Aside from being an amazing sister, daughter, friend, her best role in life is being a mother to Mila. Ever since Mila was born, she became more motivated. She worked her fingers to the bone, just so she can provide for her daughter and give her a better life. At times it's hard for her and seems like she's reached her breaking point, but she pushes herself. Mila is her world.

    My sister has had her fair shares of unfortunate events, bad choices and I'm sure she has hit rock bottom a few times. But even after all the hardship and scrutiny she received from friends and family including myself, she managed to get her life back on track. She has a stable job, and completed a program for drug and alcohol abuse and became a certified counselor. She's got great relationships with her previous and current employers. She has been a caregiver for many years, a job that I personally feel is not for just anybody, it takes a lot of patience. And that's something my sister has a lot of. To her it's not just a job, she cares for her patients and their well-being. I know at times, it's tough for her, but her effort and dedication remains.

In life we are faced with obstacles, struggles, and difficult decisions. As humans we do make mistakes, mistakes that at times cannot be undone, or easily fixed. But we manage because that is our natural instinct. My sister is not perfect, neither am I, and neither are you, but that's ok because that's what makes us who we are individually. My sister Carissa, is a good and caring person. An amazing mother, daughter, and sister. She should be here in this country, with her family. The opportunities here are endless and she has got so much more to offer. And much much more memories to make with her daughter. I strongly recommend that she is not to be deported.

Sincerely;

Allysa Unlayao

EXHIBIT '22'

Additional Letters of Support

To Whom It May Concern,

My name is ███████████. I am a co-worker of ███████████████ at Alorica in Clovis, Ca. We handle customer service for a company that requires a strong work ethic and good character. ███████████ has constantly shown her excellent work ethic and excellent character. She is responsible, a great teammate, and a true friend. I'm truly grateful to recommend her for any endeavor she pursues! I absolutely recommend her for US citizenship.

Stephen Guillen

US Citizen

To whom it may concern,

I am writing this letter in regards to ███████████ and her character as a person and employee. She has worked for me for three months now and has become a vital part of my team.

She is here every day and on time. She is such a generous person. She always assists her peers and just overall a very good person. She always places her needs behind everyone else's and is very hardworking and diligent employee. Having her at work is a great impact on our company. Her entire life seems to revolve around her job and being a good mother. I cannot say enough positive things in regards to how great of a person she is.

Thank you for your Time,

[signature]

CERTIFICATE OF SERVICE

Re: ████████████████████████

I, Christopher A. Reed, hereby certify that I am a resident of or employed in the County of Los Angeles, State of California over 18 years of age, not a party to the within action and that I am employed at and my business address is:

Law Offices of Brian D. Lerner, APC
3233 E. Broadway
Long Beach, CA 90803
Telephone: (562) 495-0554
Facsimile: (562) 608-8672

On December 13, 2016, I served a copy of the attached *MOTION TO CONTINUE* on the following person(s) by the following method(s):

Office of the Assistant Chief Counsel
Department of Homeland Security
606 S. Olive Street, 8th Floor
Los Angeles, CA 90014
(E-Service: LOS.OCC.E-Service@ICE.DHS.gov)

I declare under penalty of perjury that the foregoing is true and correct. Executed in Long Beach, California.

DATED: December 13, 2016

By: _____
Christopher A. Reed
Attorney at Law

ABOUT THE AUTHOR

Brian D. Lerner is an Immigration Lawyer and runs a National Immigration Law Firm for nearly 30 years. He is an attorney who is a certified specialist that might help in Immigration & Nationality Law as issued by the California State Bar, Board of Legal Specialization. Attorney Lerner is an expert in Immigration Law, Removal and Deportation, Citizenship, Waiver and Appeals.

He has been a licensed attorney since 1992 and started the Law Offices of Brian D. Lerner, APC. The immigration practice consists of Immigration and Nationality Law, and everything involved with and regarding immigration which includes citizenship, investment visas, family and employment visas, removal and deportation hearings, appeals, waivers, adjustment, consulate processing and all types of immigration and citizenship matters.

He has represented clients from all over the U.S. and in many countries around the world. One side of his practice is dedicated to keeping people in the U.S. and fighting for their immigration rights, while another side is to get people back who have been deported and removed from the U.S.

Also, there is the affirmative part of Immigration Law which Brian Lerner has helped numerous people come into the U.S. on business visas, investment visas, student visas, fiancée and marriage visas, religious visas and many more. Attorney Lerner has helped immigrants who are victims of crime and domestic violence or ones that are married to abusers.

In other words, Attorney Lerner has a firm that helps people all over the U.S. He has dedicated significant time to preparing numerous petitions and applications for you to get at a fraction of the price of hiring an attorney. He says it is the next best thing to a real attorney because they are real petitions prepared by an expert.

www.ingramcontent.com/pod-product-compliance
Lightning Source LLC
Chambersburg PA
CBHW051757200326
41597CB00025B/4592